EASY LOW-CARB SLOW COOKING

EASY LOW-CARB

Slow Cooking

A Prep-and-Go Cookbook for
Ketogenic, Paleo & Low-Carb High-Fat Diets

ROBIN DONOVAN

ROCKRIDGE
PRESS

Front cover Photography © StockFood/Andrew Scrivani

Back cover Photography © Stockfood/Rua Castilho, Stocksy/Jeff Wasserman, Stockfood/Michael Wissing.

Interior Photography © Stockfood/Maja Smend, p.2; Stockfood/Spyros Bourboulis, p.6; Stocksy/Trent Lanz, p.9; Stockfood/Michael Wissing, p.10; Stocksy/Sara Remington, p.15; Stocksy/Jeff Wasserman, p.32; Stockfood/Gräfe & Unzer Verlag/Wolfgang Schardt, p.52; Stockfood/Rua Castilho, p.76; Stockfood/Gräfe & Unzer Verlag/Thorsten Suedfels, p.96; Stockfood/Jonathan Gregson, p.124; Shutterstock/Mikhail Makovkin, p.152; Stockfood/Gräfe & Unzer Verlag/Coco Lang, p.172; Stocksy/Sara Remington, p.188.

ISBN: Print 978-1-62315-771-5 | eBook 978-1-62315-772-2

For my loves,
Doug and Cashel

CONTENTS

Introduction

Y ou're home from work, tired and hungry at the end of a hard day, with a refrigerator full of food—but turning those ingredients into a healthy meal is the last thing you want to think about. How much easier it would be to stop for takeout on the way home, order delivery, or even pop a frozen dinner in the microwave! But what if you could change that and come home to a hot, healthy, home-cooked meal that's ready to eat the minute you walk in the door? A slow cooker makes that dream a reality.

I fell in love with my slow cooker when I had a job that required long hours in an office. My first slow cooker was a gift from my well-meaning mom, who worried that long days at work were forcing me to compromise my usually healthy diet. I was immediately intrigued by the idea of putting a bunch of raw ingredients in it before heading out the door and coming home to a fully prepared meal. Once I tried it I was smitten.

These days, as a work-at-home writer and recipe developer with a family to feed, the promise of a hot, home-cooked meal ready at the end of the day is even more alluring. And because I struggle to keep my weight within a healthy range, having delicious *low-carb food* at the ready is especially appealing. As anyone who has ever committed to a low-carb eating plan can attest, eating this way all day, every day isn't easy. Anything that can lessen the work, and offer a variety of appetizing menu choices, is a true gift.

Since you're holding this book, you likely already follow a low-carb diet or have been advised to begin one to shed excess weight or moderate your blood glucose levels. So, you know that eating a low-carb diet isn't always easy. Grabbing a quick bite is hard when you can't eat bread or crackers, pizza, pasta, or last night's

leftovers over rice. Cooking your own meals becomes essential when you commit to a low-carb diet, and using a slow cooker can take a lot of stress out of preparing meals. And the best thing is that with good recipes, you don't have to give up eating delicious foods to stick to your low-carb plan.

In this book, I present a variety of super-easy-to-prepare recipes for delicious, satisfying, fix-it-and-forget-it dishes to make any day of the week—most requiring no precooking and no more than 15 minutes of prep time. All recipes are suitable for people following ketogenic and low-carbohydrate diet plans. Many recipes are also suitable for those following a paleo diet. You'll find plenty of recipes for classic comfort foods adapted to reduce carbs, recipes that turn simple ingredients into delicious low-carb dishes you might never have thought of cooking in a slow cooker, and lots of family-friendly fare.

ONE
Easy Meals for Carb-Conscious Families

There's no denying that slow cookers offer convenience, but the low-and-slow cooking method can be pressed into service to make meals that are not only convenient, but also deeply satisfying and delicious. The gentle heat of a slow cooker allows you to simmer food for hours without overcooking it. It can help bring out and meld the flavors of foods, tenderize meats and hearty vegetables, and transform a handful of ingredients into a balanced, cohesive, and delicious dish. Slow cookers are the best appliance for making soups and broths packed with flavor, turning inexpensive cuts of meat into delicious stews, and transforming vegetables into nutritious meals. When you commit to a low-carb diet, the slow cooker helps you turn ingredients that require extensive cooking, such as meats and hearty vegetables, into satisfying meals with very little effort.

A LOW-CARB, HIGH-FAT DIET WITH CLEAN INGREDIENTS

Low-carbohydrate diets limit the quantity of carbs you can eat each day. The science of how and why low-carb diets work is complicated and involves several mechanisms. On a very basic level, however, restricting carbs is a way of forcing your body to burn its fat stores for energy. The digestive system breaks down dietary carbohydrates into simple sugars (glucose) that are absorbed into the bloodstream. Glucose is the fuel your body uses for all its functions, from breathing to running a marathon. When your body gets more glucose than it needs for fuel, the excess is stored in your fat cells as glycogen. By limiting the carbohydrates you consume, your body is forced to tap into your fat cells to access glycogen for energy.

By limiting the carbohydrates in your diet, you keep your blood sugar at stable levels, which increases insulin sensitivity. Because insulin plays a significant role in signaling hunger and satiety, the result is that you can eat fewer calories without feeling hungry all the time. Substituting fat calories for carbohydrate calories also helps regulate the hormones that trigger hunger. So, a low-carb, high-fat diet is great for both weight loss and managing certain conditions, such as insulin resistance and type 2 diabetes.

Low-carb diets have soared in popularity in recent years thanks to several factors. For one thing, many people lose more weight faster on a low-carb diet than on a low-fat one. These diets are fairly easy to follow, since they don't entail calorie counting or detailed tracking, and people who use them say their cravings for carbohydrates quickly diminish and their energy increases. Furthermore, low-carb diets allow certain foods, such as red meat, cheese, cream, and other delicious but high-fat foods, that are off limits on low-fat diets. And these diets have been shown in numerous studies to improve health markers, such as blood triglycerides, HDL cholesterol, blood sugar, and blood pressure.

The Four Most Common Low-Carb Diets

There are many different low-carb diet plans you can follow. While these diets differ in various ways, the one thing they have in common is they severely restrict dietary carbohydrates and rely on protein and fats, in varying proportions, for the majority of daily calories. By restricting carbohydrates, they help regulate blood sugar and insulin levels in the body, keeping energy levels stable and reducing hunger and cravings.

LOW-CARB, HIGH-FAT DIET

The low-carb, high-fat diet is exactly what it sounds like. Carbohydrates are strictly limited to stabilize blood sugar and force the body to burn its fat stores for energy. High-fat foods, such as cheese, butter, eggs, avocados, nuts, seeds, coconut oil, and fatty meats, make up the calories lost by cutting out most carbs—and keep you feeling satiated. Protein levels are kept moderate because excess protein in the diet can end up being converted to glucose, defeating the purpose of limiting your carb intake.

KETOGENIC DIET

The keto diet is a low-carb, high-fat, moderate-protein diet with the goal of putting your body into a state of "ketosis," in which, deprived of its normal quick energy source (glucose from carbohydrates), it burns fat for energy instead. A standard keto diet allows 20 to 50 net grams of carbohydrates per day, with moderate protein and lots of fat, especially from grass-fed beef and other meats; full-fat dairy products, such as butter, cream, and cheese (especially from grass-fed cows); avocados; nonhydrogenated lard or beef tallow; olive oil, coconut oil, coconut butter, and red palm oil; and peanut butter. Ideally, 75 percent of your daily calories will come from fats like those listed, 20 percent from protein (other meats, fish, dairy products, nuts, and seeds), and 5 percent from carbohydrates (vegetables, nuts, and dairy). Refined carbohydrates (sugar and other sweeteners), grains (wheat, rice, and oats), foods made from grain flours (breads, pastas, and cereals), starchy vegetables (corn, potatoes, beans, and legumes), and most fruits are off limits. *All recipes in this book adhere to ketogenic diet guidelines.*

ATKINS DIET

The Atkins diet is also a low-carb, high-fat diet, but it allows higher quantities of protein. The Atkins diet is followed in phases. The first phase, known as "induction," is very low in carbs and designed to put you into ketosis. In the second and third phases, carbs, including some fruits and whole grains, are gradually reintroduced. Like the keto diet, Atkins eschews refined carbs and sugars.

PALEO DIET

This diet is meant to mimic the way our pre-agricultural hunter-gatherer ancestors ate. Although the paleo diet's goal isn't necessarily to limit carbs, it does forbid all refined sugars, grains, legumes, and starchy vegetables, so, by default, it is a fairly low-carb diet. The diet also eliminates dairy products (except for ghee, or clarified butter) and processed foods.

Nutritional Information

A healthy low-carb, high-fat diet relies on whole, unprocessed foods. The ingredients used in this book are whole, unrefined, and without artificial additives or preservatives. Additionally:

Protein

Moderate amounts of protein should come from high-quality sources—organic, pasture-raised, and grass-fed meat; wild-caught fish and game; pastured eggs and poultry; and whole nuts and seeds or all-natural (no sugar added) nut and seed butters.

Carbohydrates

While carbohydrates are extremely limited, you need some carbs in your diet to ensure you get enough fiber and certain nutrients.

Fruit

Limit fruits to low-sugar varieties, such as berries and citrus.

Fat

Fats are extremely important to the success of a ketogenic diet, so be sure to include generous amounts in every meal. Fat can come from animal sources (fish, meat, eggs, full-fat dairy products, lard and beef tallow) or from vegetarian sources (coconut oil and butter; avocados and avocado oil; nuts and seeds, as well as nut or seed oils and butters).

Vegetables

Low-sugar, low-starch vegetables (such as leafy greens, broccoli, Brussels sprouts, cabbage, cauliflower, celery, cucumbers, radishes, and zucchini) are ideal.

Total Carbs vs Net Carbs

There are two numbers you'll see bandied about related to carbohydrates. One is **total carbs** and the other is **net carbs** (carbs minus fiber). Fiber is not digested and converted to glucose, so it doesn't affect blood sugar. When calculating your carb intake, you subtract the total fiber from the total carbohydrates to get the *net carbs*. For instance, if 1 serving of broccoli has 7 grams of carbohydrates and 3 grams of fiber, then 1 serving has a net carbohydrate count of 4 grams. On a ketogenic diet, the goal is to keep your *net carbs* (grams of carbohydrates minus grams of dietary fiber) within 20 to 50 grams per day.

All recipes in this book include nutritional information to help you follow a low-carb, high-fat diet, but be aware that these calculations are approximate, and the actual nutritional intake of these dishes will vary. Why? Because even the best nutritional analysis can only estimate calories, grams of fat, net carbs, fiber, protein, and so on in any given recipe. When you actually cook a recipe, there will be variations based on measuring, the size of ingredients (for instance, how many calories are in an apple?), how much fat a given piece of meat has, variations in the nutritional makeup of different brands of the same ingredient, and so on. Factor in any substitutions or adjustments you make to the recipe and you can see why even the best nutritional analysis is only an estimate. But, as long as you stick to the general guidelines of the diet, careful tracking of calories or carb, fat, and protein grams shouldn't be necessary. By drastically reducing your carbohydrate intake, you will also reduce your appetite, so overeating is not likely to be an issue.

Followers of the paleo diet eat meats, eggs, nonstarchy vegetables and fruits, nuts, and seeds. Paleo dieters who want to keep their carb intake low limit fruits and natural sweeteners, such as honey, as well. Because the paleo diet includes lots of nuts, seeds, avocados, coconut oil, and coconut butter, it is generally high in fat. A reliance on meat and nuts for most calories that make up the diet makes it generally high in protein, as well. *Many recipes in this book adhere to paleo diet guidelines or offer substitution tips that will make them suitable for those following the paleo diet.*

HEALTHY LOW-CARB INGREDIENTS AND SUBSTITUTES

Following a low-carb diet can seem restrictive at first, but, fortunately, the list of allowed foods is long. It includes most meats, poultry, and fish; full-fat dairy products; high-fat plant foods, such as avocados, coconut, and nuts; natural noncaloric sweeteners; and nonstarchy, low-sugar vegetables (in limited quantities). In this section you'll find comprehensive lists of which foods to enjoy and which to avoid to keep you on track.

Foods to Enjoy

The foods in **bold** are especially well suited to the slow cooker. Meats, poultry, and heartier vegetables can stand up to the long cooking times involved in slow cooking. Because the slow cooker cooks at a low temperature over a long period of time, these foods become deliciously tender as they cook. Also, because there is no evaporation during cooking when using a slow cooker, these foods retain their juices and don't become dry, as they can in the oven or on the stove top.

CARBOHYDRATES (IN SMALL QUANTITIES)

- **Artichokes**
- Asparagus
- **Bell peppers** (especially green)
- Berries (blackberries, blueberries, raspberries, strawberries)
- Broccoli
- **Brussels sprouts**
- **Butternut squash**
- **Leafy greens** (arugula, cabbage, chard, chicory, kale, lettuce, spinach)
- **Cauliflower**

- **Celery**
- Cucumbers
- **Delicata squash**
- **Eggplant**
- **Garlic**
- **Green beans**
- Herbs (basil, cilantro, oregano, parsley, rosemary, thyme, etc.)
- Jicama
- **Leeks**
- Lemons
- Limes
- **Mushrooms**
- **Okra**
- **Onions**
- **Pumpkin**
- Radicchio
- Radishes
- **Rhubarb**
- Scallions
- **Shallots**
- Snow peas
- **Spaghetti squash**
- Spices (choose whole or ground spices without sweeteners, thickeners, or other additives)
- Summer squash
- **Tomatoes** (in limited quantities)
- **Turnips**
- Zucchini

FATS

- Avocados and avocado oil
- Nuts and seeds, which are also a good source of protein (almonds, Brazil nuts, cashews, chia seeds, flaxseed, hazelnuts, macadamias, peanuts, pecans, pistachios, pumpkin seeds, sesame seeds, sunflower seeds, walnuts); note that peanuts and almonds have high levels of omega-6 fatty acids, which you want to limit
- Nut oils (almond, hazelnut, pecan, pistachio, macadamia, walnut)
- Nut milks (almond, cashew)
- Nut butters, which are also a good source of protein (almond, cashew, hazelnut, macadamia, peanut); choose all-natural, no-sugar-added varieties
- Full-fat dairy products (butter, ghee, cheese, cream, sour cream, yogurt)
- Coconut (butter, cream, milk, oil)
- Animal fat (beef tallow, chicken fat, fish oil, lard)

- Mayonnaise; avoid brands with added sugar and other additives
- Olives and olive oil
- **Red meat**
- Eggs, which are also a good source of protein (ideally from free-range chickens)

PROTEINS

- Fish (especially wild-caught catfish, cod, flounder, halibut, mackerel, mahimahi, salmon, snapper, trout, and tuna)
- Shellfish (clams, crab, lobster, mussels, oysters, scallops, shrimp, and squid)
- **Meat** (ideally grass-fed beef, goat, lamb, pork; ham, bacon, sausage, veal, venison; avoid added sugar in cured meats)
- **Poultry** (especially dark meat; ideally pastured or organic chicken, duck, pheasant, quail, turkey)
- Nuts, seeds, nut butters, and eggs
- Tofu (organic, non-GMO)

SWEETENERS

- Blackstrap molasses
- Erythritol
- Stevia

OTHER

- Dry white wine or red wine (avoid if trying to lose weight)

Foods to Avoid

If you are following a low-carb diet, certain foods should be completely avoided. These include all grains, starchy vegetables (such as corn, peas, and potatoes), and beans/legumes. Also included on the list of no-nos are most fruits (except lemons, limes, and berries in small quantities), caloric sweeteners, artificial sweeteners, and low-fat dairy products. Use the following list to confirm your choices if you have questions.

CARBOHYDRATES

- Beets
- Breads, baked goods, cereals, and pastas made from grains
- Carrots
- Corn
- Fruit juices (except lemon and lime)
- Fruits (except berries, lemons, limes)
- Grains (amaranth, barley, buckwheat, bulgur, millet, oats, rice, rye, quinoa, sorghum, wheat, etc.)
- Parsnips
- Peas
- Potatoes
- Sweet potatoes

FATS

- Hydrogenated fats and trans fats (such as margarine)
- Refined oils (canola, corn, cottonseed, grapeseed, safflower, soybean, sunflower)

PROTEINS

- Low-fat dairy products and whole milk
- Processed meats that contain sugar, nitrates, nitrites, preservatives, or other additives
- Protein powders that contain sweeteners or other additives

SWEETENERS

- Artificial sweeteners (aspartame, sucralose, saccharine)
- Sugar and other caloric sweeteners (especially refined sugar, but also honey, maple syrup, agave syrup, and other high-carb sweeteners)

COMMON SUBSTITUTIONS

Pasta

Zucchini or summer squash spiralized or cut into "noodles," or spaghetti squash. These low-carb vegetables are a great substitute for high-carb pasta made with grains. You can still have your spaghetti with meatballs without kicking your body out of ketosis.

Tortillas

Lettuce, cabbage, kale, or chard leaves. Leafy greens hold all your taco, burrito, or wrap fillings without adding a bunch of carbs.

Potatoes

Turnips. Turnips have about 70 percent fewer carbs than potatoes but add the same heartiness to slow-cooked stews and other dishes.

Caloric Sweeteners (Corn Syrup, Honey, Maple Syrup, Sugar)

Stevia. Stevia is a naturally sweet herb that is native to South America. You can buy stevia powder or liquid stevia extract in many supermarkets or health food stores. Check the ingredients before purchasing a stevia product because many contain undesirable additives. Stevia is much sweeter than sugar, so a much smaller amount is needed when substituting for sugar. For example:

1 cup of sugar =	1 tbsp of sugar =	1 tsp of sugar =
1 teaspoon of powdered stevia	¼ teaspoon of powdered stevia	a pinch of powdered stevia
or	or	or
1 teaspoon of liquid stevia	6 to 9 drops of liquid stevia	2 to 4 drops of liquid stevia

Erythritol. Erythritol is a sugar alcohol that can be used as a natural sugar substitute. Erythritol tastes like sugar but is calorie-free and low glycemic and has no unpleasant aftertaste. It comes in granulated and powder forms, and is roughly 75 percent as sweet as sugar. Many recipes substitute an equal amount of erythritol for sugar and add about 1 teaspoon of stevia powder or extract per cup. Some commercial erythritol blends contain other sweeteners that make up for the difference in sweetness; they can be substituted equally for sugar in a recipe. As with any sugar substitute, erythritol has no nutritive value and should be consumed in moderation to avoid potential negative side effects, such as diarrhea and gas.

Flour, Cornstarch, and Other High-Carb Thickeners

Xanthan gum or guar gum. Xanthan gum and guar gum are natural thickeners derived from vegetables that act as emulsifiers and thickeners. Although made of carbohydrates, only a very small amount is needed to thicken a sauce or emulsify a salad dressing, so the carbs added to a dish are negligible. Note that xanthan gum can be derived from corn, wheat, or soy, so if you have an allergy to any of those ingredients, use guar gum instead, which is derived from a bean.

ESSENTIAL INGREDIENTS FOR LOW-CARB COOKING

Keeping your refrigerator, pantry, and spice rack stocked with low-carb ingredients will help you stick to your low-carb eating plan. The following table lists the most essential items you'll need, along with shopping and storage tips. These are great to have on hand so you can whip up a delicious, healthy, low-carb meal anytime.

Essential Refrigerator/Freezer

CATEGORY & ITEMS	SHOPPING & STORAGE TIPS
FRESH HERBS	
Basil, cilantro, chives, lavender, oregano, parsley, rosemary, sage, tarragon, thyme, etc.	Use fresh herbs within a few days of purchase. Even better, plant an herb garden so you have fresh herbs whenever you need them. *Refrigerate fresh herbs with their stems in a glass or jar of water to stay fresh as long as possible.*
CHEESE	
Full-fat varieties, including Cheddar, Monterey Jack, cream cheese, Parmesan, Gorgonzola, Roquefort, Swiss, etc.	Buy blocks or wedges rather than pre-grated, which often has added fillers and stabilizers. *Refrigerate or freeze.*
EGGS	
	Choose organic, pastured eggs when possible. *Keep refrigerated.*
DAIRY	
Full-fat dairy products, including butter, crème fraîche, cream, sour cream, and yogurt (plain)	Choose full-fat organic dairy products from grass-fed cows. Make sure the products come from cows not treated with hormones or antibiotics. *Keep refrigerated.*

FRESH PRODUCE

Assorted vegetables and fruits, including broccoli, Brussels sprouts, cabbage, cauliflower, celery, chard, cucumber, kale, lemons and limes, lettuce (including salad-in-a-bag types), onions, peppers, radishes, scallions, summer squash, tomatoes, and zucchini

Choose organic when possible and, ideally, choose produce that is grown locally and in season.

Storage varies: Tomatoes and cucumbers should be kept on the countertop. Whole, unpeeled onions should be stored in a cool, dark, dry place but refrigerated once peeled and cut. Most other vegetables should be stored in the refrigerator.

FROZEN PRODUCE

Berries, broccoli, onions, peppers, spinach

Stock up during sales so you always have vegetables to cook with, even when you don't have time to shop for fresh produce.

Keep frozen until ready to use.

MEAT, FISH, POULTRY

Beef, chicken, duck, lamb, mackerel, pork, quail, salmon, shellfish, trout, tuna, turkey, venison, etc.

Look for specials or buy frozen to save money.

Use within a few days of purchasing or freeze for long-term storage.

CURED OR PROCESSED MEATS

Bacon, Canadian bacon, ham, salami, deli meats, sausages, etc.

Check labels and avoid any with sugar, nitrates, or other undesirable additives.

Keep refrigerated.

Essential Pantry

CATEGORY & ITEMS	SHOPPING & STORAGE TIPS
DRIED HERBS AND SPICES	
Allspice, basil, black pepper, cayenne pepper, chili powder, chives, cinnamon, cloves, coriander, cumin, ginger, lavender, oregano, parsley, rosemary, sage, tarragon, thyme, turmeric, etc.	Many supermarkets sell dried herbs and spices in bulk at lower prices than the jarred variety. If you buy jarred, stick to smaller containers unless you plan to use a lot of that spice in a short time. *Store dried herbs and spices in tightly closed jars in a cool, dark place, such as a cabinet or spice drawer.*
CANNED VEGETABLES	
Artichoke hearts, green chiles, mushrooms, tomatoes	Look for organic varieties; check ingredients and avoid products containing additives, including thickeners, emulsifiers, sweeteners, and preservatives.
CANNED TOMATO PRODUCTS	
Paste, sauce, purée	Choose organic when possible.
GARLIC	
Fresh whole bulbs, minced in jars, or frozen	Check for and avoid added ingredients, such as sugar and preservatives. *Store fresh garlic in a cool, dark, dry place; peel and chop just before using.*
ONIONS	
White, yellow, red	Choose organic when possible. *Store onions in a cool, dark, dry place; peel and chop just before using.*

SALT

Kosher salt: Preferred because, unlike table salt, it is free of additives; substitute additive-free sea salt, if you like.

Fine sea salt: Baking recipes specify fine sea salt because its finer grains incorporate more easily into baked goods.

Look for additive-free salts, whether kosher salt or fine sea salt.

Store all salts in a covered container in a cool, dry place.

BROTH

Homemade or canned, bouillon cubes, or broth concentrate

Look for brands without sugar or preservatives, or make your own and freeze it in premeasured portions.

Freeze leftover or homemade broth in resealable plastic bags or ice cube trays.

COOKING OILS

Avocado, coconut, etc.

Choose organic, cold-pressed oils when possible. Avoid refined vegetable oils, such as canola, grapeseed, corn, and soybean, and any oil that has been heat expelled or chemically processed.

Store in a cool, dark place.

FINISHING OILS

Hazelnut, olive, walnut

These oils are more expensive than cooking oils and are best for salad dressings or as finishing touches to add flavor.

Store in a cool, dark place.

CANNED MEAT AND FISH

Anchovies, chicken, salmon, sardines, tuna, etc.

Choose "light," pole-caught tuna for the most environmentally sustainable option. Light skipjack tuna is also lower in mercury. Avoid yellowfin and albacore tunas, which have higher mercury levels. Choose wild-caught salmon from Alaska and avoid farmed salmon. Look for products in BPA-free cans or in pouches or jars, which are BPA-free.

Slow Cooker Safety Tips

When used correctly, slow cookers are very safe for cooking. Here are a few important safety tips to keep in mind.

Never put frozen food in the slow cooker and turn it on.

Meats and vegetables put into the pot frozen will prevent the cooker from reaching the safety zone (above 140°F) quickly enough to prevent bacteria from flourishing, which can put you at risk for food-borne illness. Always thaw meats and vegetables before putting them in a slow cooker to cook.

A slow cooker's ceramic insert can shatter when subjected to sudden temperature changes.

Always place a towel or trivet on a cold surface before placing a hot slow cooker insert on it. Similarly, if you fill your insert with raw ingredients and refrigerate it overnight, let it come to room temperature before turning on the slow cooker.

Avoid letting your food sit for more than two hours.

Leaving food in your slow cooker for extended periods of time before or after cooking can be dangerous because it keeps food in the danger zone temperature range. The USDA recommends not leaving cold food or cooked food at room temperature for longer than two hours.

Use wooden, plastic, or nonstick utensils when stirring or serving food.

Metal tools can scratch the ceramic insert, causing liquid to seep out and the insert to eventually crack.

Don't store food in the insert.

The insert is made for holding heat. If you store hot food in the insert and put it in the refrigerator, the food will take too long to cool to a safe temperature and bacteria may grow.

SLOW COOKING FOR THE LOW-CARB LIFESTYLE

I could write a whole book on what makes slow cookers such handy appliances to have in your kitchen, but plenty of others have already done that. While using a slow cooker can be a boon to any time-pressed person (and who isn't?), it is especially helpful for those following a low-carb lifestyle. For one thing, slow cooking is the cooking method of choice for many staple foods that make up a low-carb diet, especially meat. The long, moist, low-heat cooking of a slow cooker turns any meat tender and delicious, rendering even the toughest cuts fork-tender. Vegetables, too, become savory, tender, and delicious using this cooking method, especially when cooked together with meats.

Another reason slow cooking is so perfect for people following a low-carb diet is that it take a lot of the stress and effort out of making a healthy dinner—and, to stay in control of what you eat and keep carb intake low, you have to cook many of your own meals. Since preparing meals at the end of the workday can be challenging, the slow cooker offers an ideal solution. Start your meal in the morning, pop it in the slow cooker, and come home to a ready-to-eat, delicious, healthy, low-carb meal.

If those good reasons aren't enough to get on the low-carb slow-cooking bandwagon, the potential for leftovers will probably convince you. See, it's just as easy to make a lot of food in the slow cooker as a little, so you'll always have leftovers for lunch or future dinners. Just refrigerate or freeze leftovers in individual portions, and a good meal is literally minutes away.

Choosing a Slow Cooker

One of the best features of the slow cooker is that it allows you to plan ahead. Even better, many slow cookers have built-in timers that let you delay the start time so your food can be ready when you get home, without being overcooked. If you are in the market for a new slow cooker, today's options range from the basic models to those that include advanced features, such as delay timers, programmability, an automatic "keep warm" setting, and more.

A built-in timer is one of the best features of higher-end models. It allows you to set a dish to cook for, say, 6 hours and then automatically switch to the "keep warm" setting so your food doesn't overcook by the time you get home.

Even better, many slow cookers include delay timers that allow you to set up the dish before you leave and set it to start cooking at a later time. If you don't have this feature on your slow cooker, not to worry, since a standard outlet timer can be pressed into use—you plug it into your outlet, plug the slow cooker into it, and set the timer to turn the slow cooker on whenever you want. You can find outlet timers online or at home improvement stores. They come in a range of prices with a corresponding level of features. The fanciest models are remotely programmable via an app on your smart phone.

How easy is this? You prep and refrigerate ingredients the night before, in a separate container or in the slow cooker's ceramic insert. In the morning, you transfer the food or the insert to the slow cooker, but it needs to come to room temperature before you turn it on. With a built-in delay timer or an outlet timer, you can set it to turn on 30 or 45 minutes after you leave the house.

Most slow cookers cook food at a temperature around 212°F. Many allow you to choose a high or low setting. Both settings use the same cooking temperature (around 212°F), but a high setting achieves that temperature faster than a low setting. Generally speaking, the low setting cooks foods half as quickly as the high setting. So, if a recipe says to cook for 4 hours on high, you could, instead, cook it for 8 hours on low. The opposite is also true. If a dish cooks for 7 hours on low, you could cook it for 3 ½ hours on high. Note that some dishes cook better on one setting versus the other, so this rule can't always be applied without giving some thought to what the dish is. For instance, chicken, particularly white meat, often becomes dry if cooked on the high setting, so I've specified longer cook times on the low setting for most chicken dishes in the book.

Furthermore, I use longer cooking times as the default to accommodate people who want to set up their dinner before they leave for work in the morning and let it cook all day. The same strategy applies to breakfast: Load up your slow cooker before bed, and a hearty, hot meal is waiting for you when you wake up! However, if you wish to speed up the cooking, for many dishes it is fine to use the high setting instead and halve the cooking time. These recipes include a "Faster Cook Option" designation and provide instructions for both methods.

One other factor to keep in mind when deciding which slow cooker to purchase is size. Slow cookers come in a range of sizes, from 2 quarts to 8 quarts or even larger. For two adults, a 4-quart slow cooker is probably sufficient, but if you like leftovers you might want to go bigger. A 6-quart slow cooker is a good size for a family of three or four and is big enough to allow leftovers. If you have a very large family or often cook for large groups, opt for an even bigger model. The recipes in this book generally assume you are using a 4- or 6-quart slow cooker.

Recipes can be halved or doubled as needed to fit smaller or larger slow cookers. Keep in mind that the slow cooker should generally be half to two-thirds full, so adjust ingredients as needed. The cooking temperature and cooking time usually remain the same.

Practical Tips and Tricks

While slow cooking is arguably one of the easiest ways to make a meal, there are some tips and tricks that can help you achieve the best results with the least amount of effort.

1. **Keep veggies from turning to mush.** Foods cook at different rates in the same cooking environment. To ensure veggies don't turn to mush while your meat is still raw in the middle, or the zucchini doesn't suffer the same fate while your carrots remain crunchy, pay attention to the sizes you cut them into. Heartier vegetables, such as carrots, and other foods that take longer to cook, such as meats, should be cut into small pieces. More delicate foods can be left whole or cut into large pieces. Likewise, layering delicate vegetables on top of the meat in your slow cooker can help keep them from overcooking.

2. **Avoid soupiness.** When you cook food in a slow cooker, there is no evaporation as there is when you cook on a stove top or in the oven. As a result, some dishes can become soupy or watery. To avoid this, don't add more liquid than a recipe calls for, even if it doesn't seem like enough when you assemble the ingredients. Remember, many ingredients release liquid as they cook, which adds to any liquid you've added to the slow cooker. If you do end up with an abundance of sauce, you can always save it for another dish.

3. **Thaw frozen foods before cooking.** Frozen foods (vegetables or meat) are fine to cook in the slow cooker, but, for safety reasons, they should be thawed first. Putting frozen food directly into the cooker and turning it on can mean they spend too much time in the temperature "danger zone" (between 40°F and 140°F) in which bacteria flourish. Most meats and vegetables can be thawed overnight in the refrigerator. To thaw more quickly, place them (tightly wrapped or in their original, unopened packaging) in a bowl of cold water, which will thaw them in 15 to 60 minutes.

4. **Choose the right meats.** Fattier, tougher cuts of meat are the best choices for the slow cooker. Pot roasts, pork shoulder, short ribs, lamb shanks, and dark-meat poultry do especially well in the low, moist heat of a slow cooker, becoming tender and remaining juicy. Leaner meats—think pork tenderloin and chicken breast—can dry out with long cooking. Likewise, fish and shellfish, which tend to be lean and cook much more quickly than meat, are not good candidates for the long cooking times of the slow cooker.

5. **Use herbs and spices for flavor.** Use fresh or dried herbs and spices, as well as flavorful vegetables, such as onions, garlic, leeks, and shallots, to add deep flavor to your dishes rather than relying on packaged mixes or bottled sauces that are likely loaded with sugar, high-carb thickeners, or preservatives. Marinating meats in a bit of oil and vinegar and some herbs and spices before cooking can also add depth of flavor.

THE RECIPES

To develop the collection of recipes in this book, I took inspiration from beloved classics and adapted them to be slow-cooker and low-carb friendly. I also incorporate more modern, creative dishes that will keep you from getting bored of the low-carb lifestyle. All recipes are delicious, satisfying, and compatible with a ketogenic diet. That means they are very low in carbs, moderate in protein, and high in fat. The only exceptions are a few condiments, sauces, and stocks, which are low in carbs but not necessarily high in fat. It is assumed these will be combined with high-fat ingredients to make a meal, rather than eaten on their own. Many recipes are also naturally suitable for those following a paleo diet. Those that aren't often include variations or substitution tips that make them appropriate.

I believe anyone, even the busiest or cooking-challenged among us, can follow a healthy low-carb diet, and the slow cooker helps. All recipes, except for a few breakfast dishes, sweets, condiments or sauces, and those made ahead in bulk, can be in assembled in the morning and cooked in the slow cooker for 6 hours or longer so you come home to a hot, nourishing meal at the end of the day.

To help you decide what might be best to cook on any particular day, I use the following recipe labels throughout the book:

- **Quick Prep.** Recipes that require 15 minutes or less to prep for cooking.

- **Faster Cook Option.** Recipes can be cooked at a higher temperature for a shorter amount of time, making them convenient for people who don't want to wait all day for a meal. For these recipes, both options are given in the instructions.

- **Make It Allergen-Free.** Recipes include substitution tips for any of the "big 8" allergens (milk, eggs, fish, crustaceans, tree nuts, peanuts, wheat, soybeans) used in the dish.

- **Paleo Friendly.** Recipes are suitable as written for those following a paleo diet, or include tips to make the dish suitable for the paleo diet.

- **Worth the Effort.** Recipes require a little extra work, either before or after cooking, but are special enough to merit the extra effort.

- **Make Ahead in Bulk.** Recipes may not take a full day of uninterrupted slow cooking to prepare, but they can be made in larger quantities—say, on the weekend—and used throughout the week or frozen for longer-term storage.

TWO
Breakfast & Brunch

Macronutrients
Fat 70%
Protein 20%
Carbs 10%

Per Serving
Calories: 310
Total fat: 25g
Protein: 17g
Total carbs: 9g
Fiber: 4g
Net carbs: 5g
Sodium: 1,292mg
Cholesterol: 471mg

Greek Frittata with Olives, Artichoke Hearts & Feta

Serves 6 • Prep: 10 minutes • Cook: 6 hours on low or 3 hours on high

The slow cooker makes great frittatas—tender and full of flavor. Frittatas are delicious when served hot, right out of the cooker, or at room temperature, so leftovers make a great take-to-work lunch. This version is loaded with Greek flavors, from salty olives and feta to roasted red peppers and artichoke hearts.

1 tablespoon unsalted butter, Ghee (page 179), or extra-virgin olive oil

½ (14-ounce) can artichoke hearts, drained and diced

½ (12-ounce) jar roasted red bell peppers, drained and diced

½ cup pitted Kalamata olives, drained and halved

4 scallions (both white and green parts), sliced

12 large eggs

2 tablespoons heavy (whipping) cream

1 tablespoon minced fresh oregano or 1 teaspoon dried oregano

½ teaspoon kosher salt

¼ teaspoon freshly ground black pepper

8 ounces crumbled feta cheese

1. Generously coat the inside of the slow cooker insert with the butter.

2. Layer the artichoke hearts in the bottom of the cooker. Next, layer the roasted bell peppers, then the olives, and finally the scallions.

3. In a large bowl, beat the eggs, then whisk in the heavy cream, oregano, salt, and pepper. Pour the egg mixture over the layered vegetables.

4. Sprinkle the feta cheese over the top. Cover and cook for 6 hours on low or 3 hours on high. Serve hot, warm, or at room temperature.

5. Slice any leftover frittata into individual serving–size pieces and refrigerate in a covered container for up to 3 days.

Variation Tip You can make a frittata with just about anything you have on hand. Substitute fresh red bell peppers for roasted, use zucchini instead of artichoke hearts, or experiment with different herbs and cheeses for variety.

Zucchini, Cherry Tomato & Ricotta Frittata

Serves 6 • Prep: 15 minutes • Cook: 6 hours on low or 3 hours on high

QUICK PREP

FASTER COOK OPTION

Macronutrients
Fat 70%
Protein 25%
Carbs 5%

Per Serving
Calories: 291
Total fat: 22g
Protein: 18g
Total carbs: 4g
Fiber: 1g
Net carbs: 3g
Sodium: 670mg
Cholesterol: 461mg

This simple frittata is loaded with summery zucchini and cherry tomatoes. It's perfect for brunch on the patio on a warm summer morning, yet simple enough to make anytime. Feel free to switch up the herbs if you like—for instance, try using fresh oregano, basil, or mint in place of the parsley and thyme.

2 medium zucchini, shredded

1 teaspoon kosher salt, divided

1 tablespoon extra-virgin olive oil

12 large eggs

3 tablespoons heavy (whipping) cream

3 tablespoons finely chopped fresh parsley

1 tablespoon fresh thyme or 1 teaspoon dried thyme

½ teaspoon paprika

½ teaspoon freshly ground black pepper

6 ounces ricotta cheese

12 cherry tomatoes, halved

½ cup grated Parmesan cheese

1. In a colander set in the sink, toss the shredded zucchini with ½ teaspoon of salt. Let the zucchini sit for a few minutes, then squeeze out the excess liquid with your hands.

2. Generously coat the inside of the slow cooker insert with the olive oil.

3. In a large bowl, beat the eggs, then whisk in the heavy cream, parsley, thyme, paprika, pepper, and the remaining ½ teaspoon of salt.

4. Add the zucchini and stir to mix well. Transfer the mixture to the prepared insert.

5. Using a large spoon, dollop the ricotta cheese into the egg mixture, distributing it evenly.

6. Top with the tomatoes and sprinkle the Parmesan cheese over the top. Cover and cook for 6 hours on low or 3 hours on high. Serve hot, warm, or at room temperature.

7. Slice any leftover frittata into individual serving–size pieces and refrigerate in a covered container for up to 3 days.

Variation Tip If you don't have cherry tomatoes, substitute a thinly sliced large tomato.

Macronutrients
Fat 70%
Protein 26%
Carbs 4%

Per Serving
Calories: 370
Total fat: 29g
Protein: 24g
Total carbs: 4g
Fiber: 1g
Net carbs: 3g
Sodium: 643mg
Cholesterol: 484mg

Frittata with Cherry Tomatoes, Asparagus & Thyme

Serves 6 • Prep: 10 minutes • Cook: 6 hours on low or 3 hours on high

This frittata gets rich flavor from sharp Cheddar and Parmesan cheeses and fresh thyme. Topped with whole cherry tomatoes, and ringed with asparagus spears, it's as beautiful as it is flavorful. Serve it hot or at room temperature, topped with a dollop of crème fraîche or sour cream, if desired.

2 tablespoons unsalted butter, Ghee (page 179), or extra-virgin olive oil

12 large eggs

¼ cup heavy (whipping) cream

1 tablespoon minced fresh thyme or 1 teaspoon dried thyme

½ teaspoon kosher salt

¼ teaspoon freshly ground black pepper

1½ cups shredded sharp white Cheddar cheese, divided

½ cup grated Parmesan cheese

16 cherry tomatoes

16 asparagus spears

1. Generously coat the inside of the slow cooker insert with the butter.

2. In the slow cooker, beat the eggs, then whisk in the heavy cream, thyme, salt, and pepper.

3. Add ¾ cup of Cheddar cheese and the Parmesan cheese and stir to mix.

4. Sprinkle the remaining ¾ cup of Cheddar cheese over the top.

5. Scatter the cherry tomatoes over the frittata.

6. Arrange the asparagus spears decoratively over the top. Cover and cook for 6 hours on low or 3 hours on high. Serve hot, warm, or at room temperature.

7. Slice any leftover frittata into individual serving–size pieces and refrigerate in a covered container for up to 3 days.

Variation Tip For even more flavor, dice 1 onion and sauté it in a hot skillet in 1 table-spoon unsalted butter until soft and translucent. Let cool slightly while you prepare the egg mixture. Stir the cooked onion into the egg mixture and proceed with the recipe.

Ham, Cheese & Broccoli Breakfast Casserole

Serves 6 to 8 • Prep: 10 minutes • Cook: 6 hours on low or 3 hours on high

This savory egg casserole is rich with cream and two kinds of cheese. Broccoli florets give it welcome texture and color, and the chunks of ham make it hearty enough to serve for dinner. This is another dish that makes great leftovers. Just pop a slice in the microwave for a quick meal.

1 tablespoon unsalted butter, Ghee (page 179), or extra-virgin olive oil

10 large eggs, beaten

1 cup heavy (whipping) cream

1½ cups shredded sharp Cheddar cheese, divided

½ cup grated Romano cheese

½ teaspoon kosher salt

¼ teaspoon freshly ground black pepper

8 ounces thick-cut ham, diced

¾ head broccoli, cut into small florets

½ onion, diced

Macronutrients
Fat 70%
Protein 24%
Carbs 6%

Per Serving
Calories: 465
Total fat: 36g
Protein: 28g
Total carbs: 7g
Fiber: 2g
Net carbs: 5g
Sodium: 1,168mg
Cholesterol: 442mg

1. Generously coat the inside of the slow cooker insert with the butter.

2. Directly in the insert, whisk together the eggs, heavy cream, ½ cup of Cheddar cheese, the Romano cheese, salt, and pepper.

3. Stir in the ham, broccoli, and onion.

4. Sprinkle the remaining 1 cup of Cheddar cheese over the top. Cover and cook for 6 hours on low or 3 hours on high. Serve hot.

Variation Tip This versatile casserole can be a great way to use up ingredients you have on hand. Substitute Canadian bacon or sausage for the ham; use different types of cheese, such as Swiss or fontina; and substitute other vegetables, such as asparagus, for the broccoli.

Macronutrients
Fat 70%
Protein 24%
Carbs 6%

Per Serving
Calories: 784
Total fat: 61g
Protein: 45g
Total carbs: 14g
Fiber: 2g
Net carbs: 12g
Sodium: 2,355mg
Cholesterol: 491mg

Huevos Rancheros

Serves 6 • Prep: 15 minutes • Cook: 6 hours on low

Traditional huevos rancheros—aka "rancher's eggs"—consists of fried eggs piled atop corn tortillas and beans and smothered in a spicy tomato-based sauce. This low-carb version has a meaty, saucy base of chorizo and salsa topped with a cheesy egg mixture. The whole thing cooks together in the slow cooker while you sleep. Serve low-carb tortillas to scoop it all up with, if you like. You can also garnish it with guacamole, additional salsa or hot sauce, sour cream, or minced fresh cilantro.

1 tablespoon coconut oil

1 pound Mexican chorizo, casings removed

1 onion, diced

2 cups salsa

10 large eggs

1 cup ricotta cheese

2 cups grated Cheddar cheese, divided

¾ cup heavy (whipping) cream or half-and-half

1 (4-ounce) can diced green chiles, drained

½ teaspoon kosher salt

1. In a large skillet, heat the coconut oil over medium heat.

2. Add the chorizo and onion and sauté until the sausage is browned and the onions are soft, about 5 minutes. Using a slotted spoon, transfer the sausage mixture to the slow cooker, leaving behind the excess fat.

3. Stir the salsa into the sausage.

4. In a large bowl, beat the eggs, then whisk in the ricotta cheese, 1 cup of Cheddar cheese, heavy cream, green chiles, and salt. Pour the egg mixture over the sausage mixture in the slow cooker.

5. Sprinkle the remaining 1 cup of Cheddar cheese over the top. Cover and cook for 6 hours on low. Serve hot.

Make It Paleo Use almond milk or another paleo milk substitute in place of the heavy cream and omit the cheeses. Top with guacamole or sliced avocado before serving.

Cauliflower–Hash Brown Breakfast Bake

Serves 6 • Prep: 15 minutes • Cook: 6 hours on low

QUICK PREP
PALEO FRIENDLY

Macronutrients
Fat 70%
Protein 25%
Carbs 5%

Per Serving
Calories: 523
Total fat: 40g
Protein: 33g
Total carbs: 7g
Fiber: 2g
Net carbs: 5g
Sodium: 1,134mg
Cholesterol: 509mg

Cauliflower makes a great substitute for starchy, high-carb potatoes in this simple breakfast casserole. Layered with sausage and cheese and held together with eggs, it is both filling and delicious. If possible, use a food processor to make quick work of shredding or mincing the cauliflower.

1 tablespoon unsalted butter, Ghee (page 179), or extra-virgin olive oil

12 large eggs

½ cup heavy (whipping) cream

1 teaspoon kosher salt, plus more for seasoning

½ teaspoon freshly ground black pepper, plus more for seasoning

½ teaspoon ground mustard

1 head cauliflower, shredded or minced

1 onion, diced

10 ounces cooked breakfast sausage links, sliced

2 cups shredded Cheddar cheese, divided

1. Generously coat the inside of the slow cooker insert with the butter.

2. In a large bowl, beat the eggs, then whisk in heavy cream, 1 teaspoon of salt, ½ teaspoon of pepper, and the ground mustard.

3. Spread about one-third of the cauliflower in an even layer in the bottom of the cooker.

4. Layer one-third of the onions over the cauliflower, then one-third of the sausage, and top with ½ cup of Cheddar cheese. Season with salt and pepper. Repeat twice more with the remaining ingredients. You should have ½ cup of Cheddar cheese left.

5. Pour the egg mixture evenly over the layered ingredients, then sprinkle the remaining ½ cup Cheddar cheese on top. Cover and cook for 6 hours on low. Serve hot.

Make It Paleo Substitute almond milk for the heavy cream, omit the cheese, and use a paleo-friendly sausage or bacon.

Macronutrients

Fat 73%

Protein 22%

Carbs 5%

Per Serving

Calories: 387

Total fat: 33g

Protein: 21g

Total carbs: 4g

Fiber: 1g

Net carbs: 3g

Sodium: 675mg

Cholesterol: 302mg

Crustless Smoked Salmon & Asparagus Quiche

Serves 6 • Prep: 15 minutes • Cook: 6 hours on low or 3 hours on high

Salmon is a great source of protein and is loaded with omega-3 fatty acids. Added to a crustless quiche, along with cheese, eggs, and cream, it makes a very special breakfast or brunch dish that's easy enough—and healthy enough—to eat every day.

1 tablespoon extra-virgin olive oil

6 large eggs

1 cup heavy (whipping) cream

2 teaspoons chopped fresh dill, plus additional for garnish

½ teaspoon kosher salt

¼ teaspoon freshly ground black pepper

1½ cups shredded Havarti or Monterey Jack cheese

12 ounces asparagus, trimmed and sliced

6 ounces smoked salmon, flaked

1. Generously coat the inside of the slow cooker insert with the olive oil.

2. In a large bowl, beat the eggs, then whisk in the heavy cream, dill, salt, and pepper.

3. Stir in the cheese and asparagus.

4. Gently fold in the salmon and then pour the mixture into the prepared insert. Cover and cook for 6 hours on low or 3 hours on high. Serve warm, garnished with additional fresh dill.

Make It Paleo Substitute full-fat coconut milk or almond milk for the heavy cream and omit the cheese. Add a couple extra eggs if you like.

Sausage, Squash & Pepper Hash

Serves 4 • Prep: 10 minutes • Cook: 6 hours on low

QUICK PREP
PALEO FRIENDLY

Macronutrients
Fat 70%
Protein 20%
Carbs 10%

Per Serving
Calories: 502
Total fat: 38g
Protein: 27g
Total carbs: 12g
Fiber: 2g
Net carbs: 10g
Sodium: 1,351mg
Cholesterol: 93mg

This meaty hash substitutes bright butternut squash for the usual starchy white potatoes, making it both more nutritious and lower in carbs. Serve it on its own or top with poached or fried eggs.

2 tablespoons extra-virgin olive oil

14 ounces smoked chicken sausage, halved lengthwise and thinly sliced crosswise

¼ cup chicken broth

1 onion, halved and sliced

½ medium butternut squash, peeled, seeds and pulp removed, and diced

1 small green bell pepper, seeded and cut into 1-inch-wide strips

½ small red bell pepper, seeded and cut into 1-inch-wide strips

½ small yellow bell pepper, seeded and cut into 1-inch-wide strips

2 teaspoons snipped fresh thyme or ½ teaspoon dried thyme, crushed

½ teaspoon kosher salt

½ teaspoon freshly ground black pepper

1 cup shredded Swiss cheese

1. In the slow cooker, combine the olive oil, sausage, broth, onion, butternut squash, bell peppers, thyme, salt, and pepper. Toss to mix. Cover and cook for 6 hours on low.

2. Just before serving, sprinkle the Swiss cheese over the top, cover, and cook for about 3 minutes more to melt the cheese.

Make It Paleo Omit the cheese, and use a paleo-friendly sausage or diced ham.

Macronutrients
Fat 71%
Protein 25%
Carbs 4%

Per Serving
Calories: 779
Total fat: 61g
Protein: 50g
Total carbs: 8g
Fiber: 2g
Net carbs: 6g
Sodium: 1,199mg
Cholesterol: 1,112mg

Sausage & Egg
Stuffed Mushrooms

Serves 6 • Prep: 15 minutes • Cook: 6 hours on low

I like to think of this as the ketogenic version of that famous fast-food breakfast muffin sandwich—only healthier! When choosing breakfast sausage, check the ingredients and avoid any with high-carb ingredients, such as maple syrup. Use any type of cheese you like for this recipe, from a mild Monterey Jack to a sharp Cheddar or Gruyère.

1 tablespoon unsalted butter, Ghee (page 179), or extra-virgin olive oil

6 large eggs

1 pound mushrooms, stems minced, caps left whole

1 pound bulk breakfast sausage, or links with casings removed

1 cup chopped fresh kale

1½ cups shredded cheese of choice (see headnote), divided

½ onion, minced

2 garlic cloves, minced

⅓ cup chopped walnuts

½ teaspoon kosher salt

½ teaspoon freshly ground black pepper

1. Generously coat the inside of the slow cooker insert with the butter.

2. In a medium bowl, beat the eggs, then stir in the minced mushroom stems, sausage, kale, 1 cup of cheese, onion, garlic, walnuts, salt, and pepper.

3. Spoon the mixture into the mushroom caps and place each filled cap in the bottom of the slow cooker in a single layer.

4. Sprinkle the remaining ½ cup of cheese over the top. Cover the slow cooker and cook for 6 hours on low. Serve hot.

Make It Paleo Omit the cheese. After cooking, top the mushrooms with additional walnuts that have been lightly toasted and finely chopped.

Deep-Dish Cauliflower Crust Breakfast Pizza

Serves 4 • Prep: 15 minutes • Cook: 6 hours on low or 3 hours on high

It's no secret: I love pizza for breakfast. This version, made with a cauliflower crust and topped with tangy, lemon zest–spiked goat cheese, also makes a satisfying dinner, but I prefer to put the ingredients in my slow cooker before bed and enjoy it fresh and hot in the morning. This recipe calls for "riced cauliflower," which is just cauliflower chopped into small, rice-size pieces. You can do this by grating it on the large holes of a box grater or by pulsing the cauliflower in a food processor fitted with the chopping blade.

Macronutrients
Fat 68%
Protein 25%
Carbs 7%

2 large eggs

3 cups riced cauliflower

1 cup grated Parmesan cheese

8 ounces goat cheese, divided

½ teaspoon kosher salt

1 tablespoon extra-virgin olive oil

Grated zest of 1 lemon

Per Serving
Calories: 389
Total fat: 29g
Protein: 24g
Total carbs: 6g
Fiber: 2g
Net carbs: 4g
Sodium: 672mg
Cholesterol: 152mg

1. In a large bowl, beat the eggs, then stir in the cauliflower, Parmesan cheese, 2 ounces of goat cheese, and the salt until well mixed.

2. Generously coat the inside of the slow cooker insert with the olive oil.

3. Press the cauliflower mixture in an even layer around the bottom of the cooker and extending slightly up the sides.

4. In a small bowl, stir together the remaining 6 ounces of goat cheese and the lemon zest. Dollop spoonfuls onto the cauliflower crust, distributing it evenly.

5. Put the lid on the slow cooker, but prop it slightly open with a chopstick or wooden spoon. Cook for 6 hours on low or 3 hours on high, until the edges are slightly browned.

6. When finished, turn off the cooker but let the pizza sit in it for 30 minutes before serving. Serve warm.

Make It Paleo Omit the cheeses, add 2 extra eggs, and sprinkle the lemon zest over the top before cooking.

Macronutrients
Fat 77%
Protein 19%
Carbs 4%

Per Serving
Calories: 137
Total fat: 12g
Protein: 7g
Total carbs: 1g
Fiber: 0g
Net carbs: 1g
Sodium: 82mg
Cholesterol: 225mg

Overnight Pumpkin Pie Breakfast Custard

Serves 6 • Prep: 10 minutes • Cook: 6 hours on low

Sometimes all you want in the morning is a little something sweet and creamy. This is like pumpkin pie without the crust—or all those pesky carbs. It's velvety smooth, sweet, and spicy. Made in individual ramekins or mason jars, it's a festive treat to serve for a special brunch, but simple enough, to make anytime. The individual custards last up to 1 week, covered and refrigerated, so make a batch Sunday night and enjoy them all week long.

3 cups pumpkin purée

6 large eggs

¼ cup heavy (whipping) cream

2 tablespoons coconut oil

2 teaspoons pure vanilla extract

¼ cup erythritol or 2 teaspoons stevia powder

1 teaspoon ground cinnamon

1 teaspoon ground ginger

¼ teaspoon ground allspice

⅛ teaspoon ground nutmeg

Pinch kosher salt

1. Fill the slow cooker insert with 1 inch of water. Cover and turn the slow cooker on low to preheat while you prep the ingredients.

2. In a blender, combine the pumpkin, eggs, heavy cream, coconut oil, vanilla, erythritol, cinnamon, ginger, allspice, nutmeg, and salt. Process until smooth and well combined.

3. Divide the pumpkin mixture equally among 6 (½-cup) ramekins, mason jars, or yogurt jars. Carefully place the containers in the hot water in the cooker. Cover and cook for 6 hours on low.

4. Serve the custards warm, or refrigerate and serve cold.

Make It Paleo Substitute coconut cream or full-fat coconut milk for the heavy cream, and use vanilla bean paste in place of the vanilla extract.

Keto Granola

Serves 10 (makes about 5 cups) • Prep: 5 minutes • Cook: 2 hours on high

QUICK PREP

PALEO FRIENDLY

MAKE AHEAD
IN BULK

This recipe violates one of this book's rules in that you can't "fix it and forget it" while you go off to work for the day. I wanted to include it anyway, because sometimes all you want for breakfast is something crunchy, sweet, and ready to go. Make a big batch of this granola on the weekend and enjoy it all week in a bowl with almond milk or other low-carb milk substitute, stirred into plain yogurt, or by the handful as a satisfying snack. Nuts and seeds offer protein, healthy fats, fiber, and important minerals such as calcium, magnesium, manganese, and selenium. Do be careful not to overdo your nut consumption, though, as nuts are high in omega-6 fatty acids, and eating too many can contribute to inflammation and increase risk of liver damage, type 2 diabetes, and obesity.

⅓ cup coconut oil

1½ teaspoons pure vanilla extract or vanilla bean paste

1½ cups pumpkin seeds

1 cup unsweetened shredded coconut

½ cup almonds

½ cup walnuts

½ cup pecans

½ cup hazelnuts

½ cup sunflower seeds

½ cup erythritol or ½ teaspoon stevia powder

1 teaspoon ground cinnamon

1 teaspoon kosher salt

1. Set the slow cooker on high and let it preheat.

2. Put the coconut oil in the cooker. Once melted, stir in the vanilla.

3. Add the pumpkin seeds, coconut, almonds, walnuts, pecans, hazelnuts, and sunflower seeds. Stir to mix well, making sure all the ingredients are coated with coconut oil.

4. In a small bowl, stir together the erythritol, cinnamon, and salt. Sprinkle over the ingredients in the slow cooker. Cover and cook for 2 hours on high, stirring every 30 minutes.

5. Transfer the granola to a large, rimmed baking sheet and spread it out so it cools quickly. Serve immediately or store in a covered container at room temperature for up to 3 weeks.

Variation Tip For a different flavor, mix in 2 tablespoons unsweetened cocoa powder along with the sweetener.

Macronutrients

Fat 77%
Protein 13%
Carbs 10%

Per Serving

Calories: 495
Total fat: 46g
Protein: 18g
Total carbs: 12g
Fiber: 6g
Net carbs: 6g
Sodium: 245mg
Cholesterol: 0mg

BREAKFAST & BRUNCH

Macronutrients
Fat 80%
Protein 10%
Carbs 10%

Per Serving
Calories: 213
Total fat: 20g
Protein: 6g
Total carbs: 6g
Fiber: 3g
Net carbs: 3g
Sodium: 172mg
Cholesterol: 69mg

Grain-Free Zucchini Bread

Serves 12 • Prep: 15 minutes • Cook: 6 hours on low or 3 hours on high

This grain-free, sugar-free, low-carb zucchini bread is surprisingly moist and flavorful. Xanthan gum helps hold things together in the absence of gluten, but it is optional. The bread will just be a bit more crumbly if you leave it out. This hearty bread makes a quick breakfast, spread with a bit of butter or cream cheese, or a satisfying snack.

⅓ cup unsalted butter, melted and cooled slightly, plus more for coating the pan

1 cup almond flour

⅓ cup coconut flour

2 teaspoons ground cinnamon

1½ teaspoons baking powder

½ teaspoon baking soda

½ teaspoon fine sea salt

½ teaspoon xanthan gum (optional)

3 large eggs

1½ teaspoons pure vanilla extract

1 cup erythritol

1 teaspoon stevia powder

2 cups shredded zucchini

½ cup chopped walnuts or pecans

1. Generously coat a loaf pan with butter. (An 8-by-4-inch loaf pan fits nicely in my oval 6-quart slow cooker. Make sure your pan fits in the cooker before starting. No loaf pan? No problem. Use a round cake pan. Just fill it only about half to two-thirds full so the loaf has room to rise.)

2. In a medium bowl, stir together the almond flour, coconut flour, cinnamon, baking powder, baking soda, sea salt, and xanthan gum (if using).

3. In a large bowl, beat the eggs, then whisk in the melted butter, vanilla, erythritol, and stevia.

4. Stir the dry ingredients into the egg mixture.

5. Gently fold in the zucchini and walnuts.

6. Transfer the batter to the prepared loaf pan and spread it into an even layer with a rubber spatula or the back of a spoon.

7. Wad four pieces of aluminum foil into balls and put them on the bottom of the slow cooker insert. Place the filled loaf pan on top of the foil balls. (The foil balls should keep the pan raised about ½ inch from the bottom of the slow cooker so the pan doesn't get too hot.) Cover and cook for 6 hours on low or 3 hours on high.

8. Remove the pan from the slow cooker and invert the loaf onto a cooling rack. Let cool completely. Wrap in foil or plastic wrap and refrigerate. Slice and serve chilled.

Make It Paleo Substitute coconut oil for the butter, both for coating the pan and in the batter, and use vanilla bean paste in place of the vanilla extract. Substitute coconut sugar for the erythritol.

Macronutrients
Fat 77%
Protein 13%
Carbs 10%

Per Serving
Calories: 459
Total fat: 42g
Protein: 16g
Total carbs: 12g
Fiber: 6g
Net carbs: 6g
Sodium: 111mg
Cholesterol: 91mg

Cinnamon Crunch Coffee Cake

Serves 12 • Prep: 10 minutes • Cook: 3 hours on low

This is another recipe that doesn't follow the "set it and forget it while you are out for the day" rule in that it takes only about 3 hours to cook on low, but what's a breakfast and brunch chapter without a coffee cake recipe? This one is sweet and light, with a crunchy cinnamon topping. Enjoy it with a cup of coffee or tea and some fresh berries on the side.

FOR THE TOPPING

½ cup chopped walnuts

¼ cup coconut oil, melted

¼ cup erythritol

1 tablespoon ground cinnamon

¼ teaspoon stevia powder

TO MAKE THE TOPPING

In a small bowl, stir together the walnuts, coconut oil, erythritol, cinnamon, and stevia. Set aside.

Variation Tip To make this coffee cake even more scrumptious, make a cinnamon syrup to drizzle over the top. In a small saucepan over medium heat, combine ½ cup erythritol, ⅓ cup water, 1 tablespoon ground cinnamon, 1 teaspoon stevia powder, 2 tablespoons unsalted butter, and 1 teaspoon vanilla extract. Heat, stirring, until the butter melts. Drizzle the syrup over the cake before serving.

FOR THE CAKE

Coconut oil, for coating the parchment paper

3 cups almond flour

1 cup erythritol

¼ cup unflavored, unsweetened protein powder

2 teaspoons baking powder

¼ teaspoon fine sea salt

4 large eggs, at room temperature, lightly beaten

½ cup unsweetened almond milk

½ cup (1 stick) unsalted butter or Ghee (page 179), melted and cooled slightly

1 teaspoon pure vanilla extract

1 teaspoon ground cinnamon

¼ teaspoon stevia powder

TO MAKE THE CAKE

1. Line the slow cooker insert with a sheet of parchment or wax paper long enough to make a sling that will help you remove the cake when done. Coat the parchment paper with coconut oil.

2. In a large bowl, stir together the almond flour, erythritol, protein powder, baking powder, and sea salt.

3. Add the eggs, almond milk, melted butter, vanilla, cinnamon, and stevia. Beat until well combined. Transfer the batter to the slow cooker, smoothing the top with a rubber spatula.

4. Sprinkle the topping over the batter. Cover and cook for 3 hours on low. Let cool for at least 30 minutes before removing from the slow cooker.

5. Remove the cake using the parchment as a sling. Slice and serve. This cake will keep for several days in an airtight container on the countertop, or in the freezer for up to 3 months.

Macronutrients
Fat 76%
Protein 14%
Carbs 10%

Per Serving
Calories: 207
Total fat: 18g
Protein: 7g
Total carbs: 6g
Fiber: 2g
Net carbs: 4g
Sodium: 269mg
Cholesterol: 232mg

Grain-Free Pumpkin Loaf

Serves 12 • Prep: 15 minutes • Cook: 6 hours on low or 3 hours on high

With more eggs and less flour than the Grain-Free Zucchini Bread (page 46), this loaf is lighter and more cakelike. Slathered with butter or peanut butter, it makes a satisfying breakfast. On its own it's a perfect snack. Drizzled with Rich Caramel Sauce (page 186), it's a decadent dessert. You can substitute mashed butternut squash for the pumpkin or add chopped nuts, if you like.

½ cup (1 stick) unsalted butter, melted and cooled slightly, plus more for coating the pan

12 large eggs

1 cup pumpkin purée

1½ teaspoons pure vanilla extract

1 cup erythritol

2 teaspoons ground cinnamon

1 teaspoon stevia powder

1 teaspoon fine sea salt

1 cup coconut flour

1 teaspoon baking powder

1. Generously coat a loaf pan with butter. (An 8-by-4-inch loaf pan fits nicely in my oval 6-quart slow cooker. Make sure your pan fits in the cooker before starting. No loaf pan? No problem. Use a round cake pan. Just fill it only about half to two-thirds full so the loaf has room to rise.)

2. In a large bowl, beat the eggs, then whisk in the pumpkin, melted butter, vanilla, erythritol, cinnamon, stevia powder, and sea salt until combined.

3. Add the coconut flour and baking powder and beat until smooth.

4. Transfer the batter to the prepared loaf pan and spread it into an even layer with a rubber spatula or the back of a spoon.

5. Wad four pieces of aluminum foil into balls and put them on the bottom of the slow cooker insert. Place the filled loaf pan on top of the foil balls. (The foil balls should keep the pan raised about ½ inch from the bottom of the cooker so the pan doesn't get too hot.) Cover and cook for 6 hours on low or 3 hours on high.

6. Remove the pan from the slow cooker and invert the loaf onto a cooling rack. Let cool completely. Wrap in foil or plastic wrap and refrigerate. Slice and serve chilled.

Make It Paleo Substitute coconut oil for the butter (both for coating the pan and in the batter), use vanilla bean paste in place of the vanilla extract, and use homemade pumpkin purée rather than canned. You can substitute coconut sugar, honey, maple syrup, or another paleo-friendly sweetener for the erythritol.

THREE
Soups, Stews & Chili

Macronutrients

Fat 77%

Protein 16%

Carbs 7%

Per Serving
Calories: 373
Total fat: 33g
Protein: 14g
Total carbs: 7g
Fiber: 1g
Net carbs: 6g
Sodium: 226mg
Cholesterol: 123mg

Cream of Chicken Soup

Serves 6 • Prep: 10 minutes • Cook: 6 to 8 hours on low

Don't worry. This soup is miles away from the gloppy, additive-laden stuff that comes out of a can. Using just a handful of ingredients—mainly cream, chicken broth, and chicken, plus some seasonings—this super-simple recipe produces a really satisfying and tasty soup.

8 ounces boneless, skinless chicken thighs

3 cups chicken broth

¼ cup (½ stick) unsalted butter, cubed

½ small onion, diced

2 garlic cloves, minced

1 teaspoon kosher salt

½ teaspoon freshly ground black pepper

1¼ cups heavy (whipping) cream

1. In the slow cooker, combine the chicken, chicken broth, butter, onion, garlic, salt, and pepper. Cover and cook for 6 to 8 hours on low.

2. Remove the chicken from the soup and chop or shred it. Stir the chicken back into the soup, along with the heavy cream. Serve hot.

Make It Allergen-Free/Paleo Substitute full-fat coconut milk for the heavy cream. If you don't want the coconut flavor, use another milk substitute, such as almond milk (paleo) or rice milk (allergen-free).

Cheesy Cauliflower Soup

Serves 6 • Prep: 15 minutes • Cook: 6 to 8 hours on low

This rich, cheesy cauliflower soup is velvety smooth and so satisfying. Puréeing the soup is simple if you have an immersion blender. Even if you have to transfer it in batches to a countertop blender, you'll love the result.

5 cups chicken broth

1 head cauliflower, cut into chunks

1½ leeks (white and pale green parts), halved lengthwise and thinly sliced crosswise

2 garlic cloves, minced

¾ teaspoon kosher salt

½ teaspoon freshly ground black pepper

3½ cups shredded sharp Cheddar cheese

1 cup heavy (whipping) cream

1 teaspoon coconut oil

2 tablespoons snipped fresh chives

1. In the slow cooker, combine the chicken broth, cauliflower, leeks, garlic, salt, and pepper. Cover and cook for 6 to 8 hours on low.

2. Using an immersion blender or countertop blender, purée the soup until smooth, working in batches, if needed.

3. Stir in the Cheddar cheese, heavy cream, and coconut oil.

4. Serve topped with the chives.

Variation Tip To make this soup extra special, cook several bacon slices until browned and crisp. Drain on paper towels, then crumble the bacon and use it to garnish the soup.

Macronutrients
Fat 70%
Protein 20%
Carbs 10%

Per Serving
Calories: 508
Total fat: 40g
Protein: 24g
Total carbs: 15g
Fiber: 2g
Net carbs: 13g
Sodium: 1,019mg
Cholesterol: 130mg

SOUPS, STEWS & CHILI

Macronutrients
Fat 71%
Protein 15%
Carbs 14%

Per Serving
Calories: 455
Total fat: 37g
Protein: 17g
Total carbs: 15g
Fiber: 2g
Net carbs: 13g
Sodium: 653mg
Cholesterol: 98mg

Curried Broccoli, Cheddar & Toasted Almond Soup

Serves 6 • Prep: 10 minutes • Cook: 6 hours on low or 3 hours on high

This creamy, cheesy broccoli soup is a great way to use up broccoli stems. Slow cooking makes them very tender, so they blend beautifully into the creamy soup base. Toasted almonds, cooked in the soup, provide body and flavor, as well as added protein and healthy fats.

2 tablespoons unsalted butter, cubed

8 ounces broccoli stems, peeled and chopped

½ onion, diced

2 garlic cloves, minced

½ cup sliced toasted almonds, divided

6 cups Vegetable Broth (page 176) or chicken broth

1 tablespoon curry powder

Kosher salt

Freshly ground white pepper

¾ cup heavy (whipping) cream

1 ½ cups shredded sharp white Cheddar cheese

½ cup sour cream

1. In the slow cooker insert, combine the butter, broccoli, onion, garlic, ¼ cup of almonds, broth, and curry powder. Season with salt and pepper. Cover and cook for 6 hours on low or 3 hours on high.

2. Stir in the heavy cream, then stir in the Cheddar cheese by the handful until thoroughly melted and incorporated. Use an immersion or countertop blender to purée the soup until smooth, working in batches if necessary.

3. Serve hot, garnished with the sour cream and the remaining ¼ cup of almonds.

Variation Tip You can substitute almond butter for the almonds. Stir the almond butter into the soup after the cooking time is up, before puréeing the soup.

Chicken Chowder with Bacon

Serves 6 • Prep: 15 minutes • Cook: 8 hours on low

QUICK PREP

WORTH THE
EFFORT

This hearty soup isn't a true chowder because it doesn't have potatoes in it, but I promise you won't miss them. This recipe calls for precooking the bacon, which is important both to get the right texture for the bacon and to keep the soup from being greasy. I've also included a variation tip that allows you to skip this step, if you like.

12 ounces bacon

4 tablespoons (½ stick) unsalted butter or Ghee (page 179), at room temperature, divided

12 ounces boneless, skinless chicken breast, diced

6 ounces cremini mushrooms, sliced

2 celery stalks, diced

1 leek (white and pale green parts), halved lengthwise and thinly sliced crosswise

1 onion, thinly sliced

1 shallot, finely chopped

4 garlic cloves, minced

1 tablespoon minced fresh thyme

1 teaspoon kosher salt

1 teaspoon freshly ground black pepper

2 cups chicken broth

1 cup heavy (whipping) cream

8 ounces cream cheese, at room temperature

Macronutrients
Fat 70%
Protein 22%
Carbs 8%

Per Serving
Calories: 573
Total fat: 45g
Protein: 31g
Total carbs: 12g
Fiber: 1g
Net carbs: 11g
Sodium: 1,493mg
Cholesterol: 193mg

1. In a large skillet, cook the bacon over medium heat until crisp. Transfer to a paper towel–lined plate to drain. Crumble into small pieces and set aside.

2. Spread 2 tablespoons of butter over the bottom of the slow cooker insert.

3. Add the chicken, cooked bacon, mushrooms, celery, leek, onion, shallot, garlic, thyme, salt, and pepper.

4. In a medium bowl, whisk together the chicken broth, heavy cream, cream cheese, and remaining 2 tablespoons of butter until well combined and smooth. Pour the mixture over the ingredients in the slow cooker and stir to mix. Cover and cook for 8 hours on low. Serve hot.

Variation Tip If precooking the bacon seems like too much trouble, substitute diced ham or smoked pork sausage instead. (I like spicy andouille sausage, Spanish chorizo, or linguiça, but any smoked sausage will do.)

Macronutrients
Fat 65%
Protein 25%
Carbs 10%

Per Serving
Calories: 662
Total fat: 48g
Protein: 41g
Total carbs: 14g
Fiber: 1g
Net carbs: 13g
Sodium: 1,799mg
Cholesterol: 180mg

Chile Relleno Soup

Serves 6 • Prep: 10 minutes • Cook: 6 hours on low

Deep-fried chiles rellenos are delicious, but not low-carb friendly. This simple soup delivers all the flavor of classic chiles rellenos—roasted green chiles, creamy cheese, and Mexican spices—without the carbs or the work of stuffing, battering, and frying the chiles.

12 ounces boneless, skinless chicken breast, diced

3 cups chicken broth

1½ cups salsa verde

2 (4-ounce) cans fire-roasted diced green chiles, with juice

2 celery stalks, chopped

1 onion, diced

4 garlic cloves, minced

1 jalapeño pepper, seeded and minced

1 tablespoon ground cumin

1 teaspoon dried oregano

½ teaspoon kosher salt

10 ounces cream cheese, cut into cubes

4 cups shredded Cheddar cheese, divided

3 tablespoons chopped fresh cilantro

1. In the slow cooker, combine the chicken, chicken broth, salsa, green chiles and their juice, celery, onion, garlic, jalapeño, cumin, oregano, and salt. Cover and cook for 6 hours on low.

2. Just before serving, stir in the cream cheese and 2 cups of Cheddar cheese until thoroughly melted and incorporated. Serve hot, garnished with the remaining 2 cups of Cheddar cheese and the cilantro.

Variation Tip If you have extra time, ladle the soup into oven-safe bowls, sprinkle the remaining Cheddar cheese on top, and heat under the broiler until the cheese is melted, browned, and bubbly, 2 to 3 minutes.

Cream of Mushroom & Chicken Soup

Serves 6 • Prep: 15 minutes • Cook: 6 hours on low

QUICK PREP

MAKE IT
ALLERGEN-FREE

PALEO FRIENDLY

This soup combines two classics—cream of mushroom and cream of chicken—into a flavorful, satisfying dish. For a thicker soup, transfer 2 cups of broth to a small bowl before adding the cream. Add 2 tablespoons xanthan gum, whisk to blend, and stir back into the soup. Cover and cook until thickened, about 10 minutes, then stir in the cream and serve.

Macronutrients
Fat 70%
Protein 20%
Carbs 10%

Per Serving
Calories: 322
Total fat: 25g
Protein: 15g
Total carbs: 8g
Fiber: 0g
Net carbs: 8g
Sodium: 307mg
Cholesterol: 107mg

1 tablespoon coconut oil

10 ounces boneless, skinless chicken thighs, cut into 1-inch chunks

Kosher salt

Freshly ground black pepper

2 tablespoons unsalted butter

2 celery stalks, diced

½ onion, diced

3 garlic cloves, minced

8 ounces cremini mushrooms, thinly sliced

4 cups chicken broth, divided

½ teaspoon dried thyme

1 bay leaf

1 cup heavy (whipping) cream

2 tablespoons chopped fresh flat-leaf parsley

1. In a large skillet, heat the coconut oil over medium-high heat.

2. Season the chicken with salt and pepper and add it to the skillet. Sauté until browned on all sides, about 5 minutes. Transfer the chicken to the slow cooker.

3. Return the skillet to medium-high heat and add the butter. When it has melted, add the celery, onion, garlic, and mushrooms and sauté until softened, about 5 minutes.

4. Add 1 cup of chicken broth to the skillet to deglaze it. Bring to a boil and cook for about 1 minute, stirring and scraping up any browned bits from the bottom. Carefully pour the mixture into the slow cooker.

5. Stir the remaining 3 cups of broth, thyme, and bay leaf into the cooker. Cover and cook for 6 hours on low.

6. Just before serving, stir in the heavy cream and parsley. Discard the bay leaf and serve hot.

Make It Allergen-Free/Paleo Substitute coconut butter for the butter and full-fat coconut milk or coconut cream for the heavy cream.

SOUPS, STEWS & CHILI

Macronutrients

Fat 70%

Protein 22%

Carbs 8%

Per Serving

Calories: 483

Total fat: 39g

Protein: 27g

Total carbs: 12g

Fiber: 2g

Net carbs: 10g

Sodium: 729mg

Cholesterol: 78mg

Thai Red Curry Chicken Soup with Coconut Milk

Serves 6 • Prep: 10 minutes • Cook: 6 hours on low

Rich coconut milk makes a soothing backdrop for spicy Thai red curry paste, which is full of herbs and spices, such as red chiles, lemongrass, kefir lime leaves, and galangal (Thai ginger). The heat level varies among the different brands, so be cautious at first, adding more as desired. To make this a bit heartier, serve it over cauliflower rice.

2 (14-ounce) cans coconut milk

2 cups chicken broth

¼ cup all-natural peanut butter

2 tablespoons red curry paste, or more for seasoning

2 tablespoons fish sauce

1¼ pounds boneless, skinless chicken thighs, cut into 1-inch pieces

1 red bell pepper, seeded and cut into ¼-inch-wide slices

1 small onion, thinly sliced

1 tablespoon minced fresh ginger

1 tablespoon freshly squeezed lime juice

¼ cup chopped fresh cilantro

1. In the slow cooker, stir together the coconut milk, chicken broth, peanut butter, curry paste, and fish sauce.

2. Add the chicken, red bell pepper, onion, and ginger. Cover and cook for 6 hours on low.

3. Just before serving, stir in the lime juice and garnish with the cilantro. Serve hot.

Make It Allergen-Free/Paleo Use a "clean" curry paste (most are naturally grain-free, but check for added sugar or preservatives, as well as shellfish if allergies are an issue). For allergen-free, use coconut aminos in place of the fish sauce and tahini for the peanut butter; for paleo, substitute all-natural almond butter for the peanut butter.

Mulligatawny Soup with Cauliflower Rice

Serves 6 • Prep: 10 minutes • Cook: 6 hours on low

QUICK PREP

MAKE IT
ALLERGEN-FREE

PALEO FRIENDLY

The word *mulligatawny* is an Anglicized version of a Tamil word meaning "pepper broth." Mulligatawny soup is an English adaptation of a traditional Indian dish. There are many variations on this flavorful soup, but it is usually a chicken broth–based, curry-spiced, creamy soup with rice and apples. In this version, riced cauliflower stands in for the traditional rice, and the soup is sweetened with a bit of erythritol instead of diced apple. To prepare the riced cauliflower, trim off the root, chop the cauliflower into chunks, and pulse in a food processor until it is the texture of rice.

6 cups chicken broth

2 cups canned coconut milk

¾ cup coconut cream

3 tablespoons curry powder

2 tablespoons erythritol

1 teaspoon kosher salt

8 ounces boneless, skinless chicken thighs, diced

1 cup riced cauliflower

3 cups baby spinach

Macronutrients
Fat 70%
Protein 17%
Carbs 13%

Per Serving
Calories: 388
Total fat: 31g
Protein: 17g
Total carbs: 14g
Fiber: 2g
Net carbs: 12g
Sodium: 405mg
Cholesterol: 38mg

1. In the slow cooker, combine the chicken broth, coconut milk, coconut cream, curry powder, erythritol, salt, chicken, and cauliflower. Cover and cook for 6 hours on low.

2. Just before serving, stir in the spinach until it is wilted. Serve hot.

Make It Allergen-Free/Paleo Use a curry powder that is wheat- and gluten-free; for paleo, substitute coconut sugar for the erythritol.

SOUPS, STEWS & CHILI

Macronutrients
Fat 70%
Protein 23%
Carbs 7%

Per Serving
Calories: 610
Total fat: 47g
Protein: 34g
Total carbs: 16g
Fiber: 2g
Net carbs: 14g
Sodium: 2,213mg
Cholesterol: 90mg

Japanese-Style Triple Pork Soup

Serves 6 to 8 • Prep: 20 minutes • Cook: 8 hours on low

This soup is reminiscent of the Japanese soup normally served with ramen noodles. Here, shredded cabbage and bean sprouts stand in for the noodles, but the flavors are as spot-on as your favorite bowl of ramen. Feel free to add ramen-style garnishes, such as halved soft-boiled eggs and thinly sliced scallions.

12 ounces boneless pork shoulder, trimmed of excess fat and cut into 2 or 3 pieces

1 teaspoon kosher salt

2 tablespoons coconut oil

4 ounces pork belly

4 bacon slices, chopped

1 onion, diced

6 garlic cloves, minced

1 (2-inch) piece fresh ginger, peeled and minced

7 cups chicken broth, divided

8 ounces cremini or button mushrooms, sliced

1 leek (white and pale green parts), halved lengthwise and thinly sliced crosswise

1 tablespoon soy sauce or tamari

¼ head napa cabbage, thinly sliced, divided

4 ounces bean sprouts, divided

1 tablespoon toasted sesame oil

1. Season the pork shoulder with the salt.

2. In a large skillet, heat the coconut oil over medium-high heat. Add the pork shoulder, pork belly, and bacon. Cook until browned on all sides, about 8 minutes. Transfer the meat to the slow cooker.

3. Return the skillet to medium-high heat and add the onion. Sauté until softened, about 3 minutes.

4. Stir the garlic, ginger, and 1 cup of chicken broth into the skillet. Cook for 1 minute, stirring and scraping up any browned bits from the bottom of the pan. Transfer the mixture to the slow cooker.

5. Add the mushrooms, leek, and remaining 6 cups of chicken broth to the cooker. Cover and cook for 8 hours on low.

6. Using tongs or a slotted spoon, transfer the pork shoulder to a bowl. Using two forks, shred the meat. Stir the shredded meat back into the broth, along with the soy sauce.

7. To serve, fill each serving bowl with a handful each of cabbage and bean sprouts. Ladle the soup, including the meat and vegetables, over the cabbage and bean sprouts. Drizzle a bit of sesame oil over the top and serve hot.

Make It Allergen-Free/Paleo If allergens are a concern, substitute coconut aminos for the soy sauce. For paleo, substitute either coconut aminos or fish sauce.

Macronutrients
Fat 70%
Protein 20%
Carbs 10%

Per Serving
Calories: 329
Total fat: 26g
Protein: 16g
Total carbs: 9g
Fiber: 2g
Net carbs: 7g
Sodium: 568mg
Cholesterol: 62mg

Beef Soup with Cabbage

Serves 6 • Prep: 20 minutes • Cook: 8 to 10 hours on low

The flavors of this soup remind me of my grandmother's stuffed cabbage. Cooking these ingredients in soup form is a whole lot easier than stuffing and rolling all those cabbage leaves—but just as delicious and comforting. Browning the beef and sautéing the onions before adding them to the pot caramelizes them and adds depth of flavor to the soup.

2 tablespoons coconut oil

8 ounces beef stew meat, diced

Kosher salt

Freshly ground black pepper

8 ounces smoked beef sausage, diced

1 onion, finely chopped

3 cups shredded cabbage

2 cups beef broth

1 (15-ounce) can tomato sauce

2 garlic cloves, minced

2 bay leaves

3 tablespoons chopped fresh parsley

1 cup sour cream

1. In a large skillet, heat the coconut oil over medium-high heat.

2. Generously season the meat with salt and pepper and add it to the skillet, along with the sausage. Cook until the meat is browned on all sides, about 6 minutes. Transfer the beef and sausage to the slow cooker.

3. Return the skillet to medium-high heat and add the onion. Sauté until softened, about 4 minutes. Transfer the onion to the slow cooker.

4. Add the cabbage, beef broth, tomato sauce, garlic, and bay leaves to the slow cooker. Cover and cook for 8 to 10 hours on low.

5. Discard the bay leaves and serve hot, garnished with the parsley and a dollop of sour cream.

Make It Allergen-Free/ Paleo Omit the sour cream garnish or substitute plain coconut yogurt, if you like.

Rustic Italian Chicken Stew

Serves 4 • Prep: 15 minutes • Cook: 7 hours on low

This simple, rustic Italian chicken stew is easy-peasy to make, but special enough to serve for company. Using chicken dark meat and skin boosts the fat content, and also ensures tender, flavorful chunks of meat. It's paleo and free of the "big 8" allergens, making it a great potluck or party dish. To crush the fennel seeds, use the side of a large chef's knife, a rolling pin, or a can or jar turned on its side and used like a rolling pin.

¼ cup extra-virgin olive oil

12 ounces whole chicken legs and thighs

1 cup chicken broth

1 cup pitted green or black olives

1 stalk celery, chopped

½ onion, diced

2 garlic cloves, minced

2 tablespoons dry white wine

1 tablespoon tomato paste

1 teaspoon fennel seeds, crushed

½ teaspoon kosher salt

1 cup heavy (whipping) cream

2 tablespoons chopped fresh parsley

1. In the slow cooker, combine the olive oil, chicken, chicken broth, olives, celery, onion, garlic, white wine, tomato paste, fennel seeds, and salt. Stir to mix. Cover and cook for 7 hours on low.

2. Just before serving, stir in the heavy cream and the parsley.

Precooking Tip Some people like to sear meat before putting it in the slow cooker because the meat develops more complex flavors. If you want to try that here, brown the chicken pieces in the olive oil for five minutes per side on medium-high heat before adding them to the slow cooker.

Macronutrients
Fat 70%
Protein 22%
Carbs 18%

Per Serving
Calories: 447
Total fat: 34g
Protein: 26g
Total carbs: 7g
Fiber: 2g
Net carbs: 5g
Sodium: 1,082mg
Cholesterol: 117mg

SOUPS, STEWS & CHILI

Macronutrients
Fat 69%
Protein 21%
Carbs 10%

Per Serving
Calories: 610
Total fat: 46g
Protein: 31g
Total carbs: 18g
Fiber: 4g
Net carbs: 14g
Sodium: 1,444mg
Cholesterol: 132mg

Chicken & Sausage Gumbo

Serves 6 • Prep: 10 minutes • Cook: 7 hours on low

Spicy smoked andouille sausage, the "holy trinity" of Cajun cooking (onions, celery, and bell peppers), and a whole bunch of Cajun spices make this hearty soup addictive. This gumbo is a bit "brothier" than the traditional version since it doesn't have any flour, but the okra helps thicken it. If you have access to fresh okra, by all means, substitute it for the frozen. Gumbo is usually served over white rice, but I like it just as much (maybe even more) over cooked cauliflower rice.

1½ pounds andouille sausage or other spicy smoked sausage, halved lengthwise and sliced crosswise

1 pound boneless, skinless chicken thighs, diced

1 (28-ounce) can diced tomatoes, with juice

2 cups chicken broth

1 (10-ounce) package frozen sliced okra, thawed

2 celery stalks, diced

1 green bell pepper, seeded and diced

1 onion, diced

3 garlic cloves, minced

2 bay leaves

1 teaspoon dried thyme

1 teaspoon dried oregano

½ teaspoon ground mustard

½ teaspoon kosher salt

¼ teaspoon freshly ground black pepper

¼ teaspoon cayenne pepper

4 scallions, thinly sliced

1. In the slow cooker, combine the sausage, chicken, tomatoes and their juice, chicken broth, okra, celery, green bell pepper, onion, garlic, bay leaves, thyme, oregano, ground mustard, salt, black pepper, and cayenne pepper. Stir to mix. Cover and cook for 7 hours on low.

2. Discard the bay leaves and serve hot, garnished with the scallions.

Variation Tip Gumbo usually includes shellfish in addition to chicken and sausage. If shellfish allergies are not a concern, add 12 ounces peeled, deveined shrimp at the end of the cooking time. Cover and cook until the shrimp is cooked through, about 5 minutes longer.

Pork Stew with Pumpkin & Peanuts

Serves 8 • Prep: 20 minutes • Cook: 8 hours on low

PALEO FRIENDLY

WORTH THE
EFFORT

Macronutrients
Fat 72%
Protein 20%
Carbs 8%

Per Serving
Calories: 492
Total fat: 41g
Protein: 24g
Total carbs: 11g
Fiber: 2g
Net carbs: 9g
Sodium: 142mg
Cholesterol: 52mg

This peanut- and pumpkin-flavored stew has a Caribbean or West African vibe to it. It makes a satisfying meal, especially served over cauliflower rice. When purchasing canned pumpkin purée, make sure to get the kind that is 100 percent pumpkin and, ideally, organic.

2 tablespoons coconut oil	1½ cups chicken broth
1½ pounds boneless pork ribs	3 cups canned coconut milk
Kosher salt	1 cup pumpkin purée
Freshly ground black pepper	¼ cup all-natural peanut butter
½ onion, chopped	¼ cup erythritol
1 garlic clove, minced	1 teaspoon freshly squeezed lime juice
1 jalapeño pepper, seeded and minced	¼ cup chopped fresh cilantro
1 teaspoon minced fresh ginger	½ cup chopped toasted peanuts

1. In a large skillet, heat the coconut oil over medium-high heat.

2. Generously season the pork with salt and pepper and add it to the skillet. Cook until browned on both sides, about 6 minutes. Transfer to the slow cooker.

3. Return the skillet to medium-high heat and add the onion, garlic, jalapeño, and ginger. Sauté until the onions are softened, about 3 minutes.

4. Stir in the chicken broth and bring to a boil. Cook for 1 minute.

5. Stir in the coconut milk, pumpkin, peanut butter, and erythritol until smooth. Pour the mixture into the slow cooker. Cover and cook for 8 hours on low.

6. Remove the meat from the slow cooker and cut it into bite-size pieces or shred it using two forks. Return the meat to the cooker.

7. Stir in the lime juice. Serve hot, garnished with the cilantro and peanuts.

Make It Paleo Substitute almond butter for the peanut butter, sliced or slivered almonds for the chopped peanut garnish, and coconut sugar for the erythritol.

SOUPS, STEWS & CHILI

Macronutrients
Fat 74%
Protein 18%
Carbs 8%

Per Serving
Calories: 577
Total fat: 48g
Protein: 24g
Total carbs: 15g
Fiber: 6g
Net carbs: 9g
Sodium: 1,204mg
Cholesterol: 110mg

Pork Chili Verde

Serves 8 • Prep: 20 minutes • Cook: 8 hours on low or 4 hours on high

This classic Mexican dish combines meaty pork with tangy tomatillos and flavorful green chiles for a satisfying stew that's naturally low-carb and paleo. If you like, serve it with low-carb tortillas.

1 (14-ounce) can tomatillos, drained and quartered

1 (4-ounce) can diced green chiles, drained

1 cup packed fresh cilantro

2 tablespoons coconut oil

1¼ pounds boneless pork shoulder, trimmed of excess fat and cut into 2 or 3 pieces

2 teaspoons kosher salt, plus more for seasoning the pork

8 bacon slices, diced

½ onion, chopped

2 poblano or Anaheim chiles, seeded and diced

5 garlic cloves, chopped

1 tablespoon ground cumin

1 teaspoon dried oregano

1 teaspoon paprika

1 teaspoon chili powder

1½ cups chicken broth

2 cups sour cream

Lime wedges, for garnish

4 ounces queso fresco

2 large avocados, peeled, pitted, and sliced

1. In a blender or food processor, process the tomatillos, green chiles, and cilantro until smooth. Pour the mixture into the slow cooker.

2. In a large skillet, heat the coconut oil over medium-high heat.

3. Season the pork with salt and add it to the skillet, along with the bacon. Cook until browned on all sides, about 5 minutes. Transfer to the slow cooker and stir it into the sauce.

4. Return the skillet to medium-high heat and add the onion. Sauté until it begins to soften, about 2 minutes.

5. Add the chiles, garlic, cumin, oregano, paprika, chili powder, and 2 teaspoons of salt to the skillet. Sauté for 1 minute more.

6. Add the chicken broth. Cook, stirring and scraping up any browned bits from the bottom of the pan, until the liquid comes to a boil. Pour the mixture into the slow cooker. Cover and cook for 8 hours on low or 4 hours on high.

7. Stir 1 cup of sour cream into the sauce. Serve hot, garnished with lime wedges, queso fresco, avocado slices, and dollops of the remaining 1 cup sour cream.

Variation Tip With a little extra effort, you can add authentic smoky flavor to this dish. Use 2 pounds fresh tomatillos, husked and quartered, in place of the canned. Before puréeing, spread the tomatillos and chiles on a baking sheet, toss with a bit of olive oil, and place them under the broiler. Broil, turning every few minutes, until charred on all sides, 10 to 15 minutes. When cool enough to handle, remove and discard the charred skins and then purée the roasted vegetables in the blender, along with the canned chiles and cilantro.

Macronutrients

Fat 76%

Protein 18%

Carbs 6%

Per Serving
Calories: 630
Total fat: 54g
Protein: 26g
Total carbs: 11g
Fiber: 2g
Net carbs: 9g
Sodium: 1,661mg
Cholesterol: 131mg

Beef Stew with Turnips

Serves 8 • Prep: 20 minutes • Cook: 9 hours on low or 4 ½ hours on high

Classic beef stew contains potatoes, a forbidden ingredient for low-carb dieters. Here turnips take their place brilliantly. Turnips have far fewer carbs than potatoes—about 70 percent less—and when they're simmered for hours with flavorful ingredients, such as beef and tomatoes, they absorb those rich flavors just like potatoes would. I like to thicken this stew by puréeing some of the cooked vegetables. This is an especially good dish to freeze in individual servings for quick meals when needed.

¼ cup coconut oil

1 ½ pounds beef stew meat, cut into 1-inch cubes

3 teaspoons kosher salt, divided

8 bacon slices, diced

2 cups beef broth

1 (14.5-ounce) can diced tomatoes, with juice

8 ounces mushrooms, sliced

4 celery stalks, diced

4 turnips, peeled and quartered

2 tablespoons tomato paste

2 tablespoons soy sauce or tamari

1 bay leaf

1 teaspoon freshly ground black pepper

2 cups sour cream

1 cup cream cheese

3 tablespoons chopped fresh parsley

1. In a large skillet, heat the coconut oil over medium-high heat.

2. Season the beef with 1 teaspoon of salt and add it to the skillet, along with the bacon. Cook until the meat is browned on all sides, about 5 minutes. Transfer to the slow cooker.

3. Add the beef broth, tomatoes and their juice, mushrooms, celery, turnips, tomato paste, soy sauce, bay leaf, pepper, and the remaining 2 teaspoons of salt. Stir to mix. Cover and cook for 9 hours on low or 4 ½ hours on high.

4. To thicken the stew, scoop out some of the vegetables with a slotted spoon and purée them in a blender or food processor, then stir the purée back into the stew, along with the sour cream and cream cheese.

5. Discard the bay leaf and serve hot, garnished with the parsley.

Make It Allergen-Free/Paleo Substitute coconut aminos for the soy sauce.

Garlicky Beef Stew with Olives & Capers

Serves 8 • Prep: 20 minutes • Cook: 9 hours on low or 4 ½ hours on high

This stew boasts distinctive Mediterranean flavors from the olives, capers, fresh rosemary, balsamic vinegar, and tomatoes—all ingredients commonly used in Italy, France, and Greece. Plus, olives add a dose of desirable monounsaturated fats.

¼ cup coconut oil

12 ounces mushrooms, sliced

1 onion, diced

3 pounds beef stew meat, cut into 1-inch cubes

1 teaspoon kosher salt, plus more for seasoning the meat

8 bacon slices, diced

2 cups beef broth

1½ cups pitted black olives, halved or quartered

1 (14.5-ounce) can diced tomatoes, with juice

¾ cup tomato sauce

¼ cup balsamic vinegar

6 garlic cloves, thinly sliced

2 tablespoons capers, drained

2 tablespoons finely chopped fresh rosemary

2 tablespoons finely chopped fresh parsley

½ teaspoon freshly ground black pepper

2 cups sour cream

FASTER COOK OPTION

Macronutrients
Fat 71%
Protein 23%
Carbs 6%

Per Serving
Calories: 716
Total fat: 57g
Protein: 39g
Total carbs: 12g
Fiber: 2g
Net carbs: 10g
Sodium: 871mg
Cholesterol: 153mg

1. In a large skillet, heat the coconut oil over medium-high heat.

2. Add the mushrooms and onion and sauté until they begin to brown, about 5 minutes. Transfer the mixture to the slow cooker.

3. Season the beef with salt and add it to the skillet, with the bacon. Cook until browned on all sides, about 8 minutes. Transfer to the slow cooker.

4. Add the beef broth to the skillet. Bring to a boil and simmer for 1 to 2 minutes, stirring and scraping any browned bits from the bottom of the pan. Transfer the broth to the slow cooker.

5. Add the olives, tomatoes and their juice, tomato sauce, balsamic vinegar, garlic, capers, rosemary, parsley, salt, and pepper. Stir to mix. Cover and cook for 9 hours on low or 4 ½ hours on high.

6. Just before serving, stir in the sour cream. Serve hot.

Variation Tip If using the faster cook option, mince the garlic to ensure it mellows in flavor with the faster cooking time.

Macronutrients
Fat 60%
Protein 30%
Carbs 10%

Per Serving
Calories: 317
Total fat: 21g
Protein: 24g
Total carbs: 10g
Fiber: 2g
Net carbs: 8g
Sodium: 299mg
Cholesterol: 75mg

Lamb Stew with Cumin & Greens

Serves 6 • Prep: 15 minutes • Cook: 6 hours on low

Meaty lamb makes a great stew. Here it is slow cooked along with leafy greens and Middle Eastern spices, such as cumin and coriander, for a flavorful one-pot meal. Lamb shoulder is an economical cut to use for stew, but you could also use a more expensive leg of lamb. This is a brothy stew that would traditionally be served over something like couscous to soak up the juices. I like to use cauliflower rice since it serves the same purpose but is low in carbs and full of nutrients.

2 pounds lamb stew meat, cut into 1-inch cubes

2 tablespoons extra-virgin olive oil

4 garlic cloves, minced

1 tablespoon ground cumin

1 tablespoon ground coriander

½ teaspoon kosher salt

¼ teaspoon freshly ground pepper

¼ teaspoon cayenne pepper

1 large onion, diced

8 ounces kale or Swiss chard, center ribs removed, leaves julienned

¾ cup chicken or beef broth

1 (28-ounce) can diced tomatoes, with juice

1. In the slow cooker, combine the lamb, olive oil, garlic, cumin, coriander, salt, black pepper, and cayenne pepper. Toss to mix and coat the lamb.

2. Layer the onion on top of the lamb, and then the greens.

3. Pour the broth and the tomatoes and their juice over the top. Cover and cook for 6 hours on low. Serve hot.

Variation Tip Instead of hearty greens such as kale and chard, you could use more delicate baby spinach. Stir it into the stew at the end of the cooking time. Cover and let cook for an additional 5 minutes to wilt the spinach.

Creamy White Chicken Chili

Serves 6 • Prep: 10 minutes • Cook: 8 hours on low

White chicken chili thickened with sour cream is a delicious way to stick to your low-carb eating plan. It's delicious on its own, but you can also serve it with all the usual chili toppings, such as shredded cheese, guacamole or sliced avocado, diced red onion, salsa, or even cooked, crumbled bacon.

Macronutrients
Fat 70%
Protein 20%
Carbs 10%

1½ pounds boneless, skinless chicken thighs

4 cups chicken broth

1½ cups diced zucchini

1 cup diced mushrooms

1 onion, diced

1 green bell pepper, seeded and diced

4 garlic cloves, minced

1 (4-ounce) can fire-roasted diced green chiles, drained

1½ teaspoons ground cumin

1 teaspoon dried oregano

½ teaspoon chili powder

¼ teaspoon cayenne pepper

½ cup sour cream

1½ cups shredded Cheddar cheese

4 scallions, thinly sliced

2 avocados, peeled, pitted, and sliced

2 tablespoons chopped fresh cilantro

Per Serving
Calories: 591
Total fat: 44g
Protein: 30g
Total carbs: 20g
Fiber: 7g
Net carbs: 13g
Sodium: 584mg
Cholesterol: 130mg

1. In the slow cooker, combine the chicken, chicken broth, zucchini, mushrooms, onion, green bell pepper, garlic, green chiles, cumin, oregano, chili powder, and cayenne. Stir to mix. Cover and cook for 8 hours on low.

2. Remove the chicken from the slow cooker and shred it using two forks. Stir the shredded meat back into the chili, along with the sour cream. Serve hot, garnished with the Cheddar cheese, scallions, avocado, and cilantro.

Make It Allergen-Free/Paleo Omit the sour cream (substitute full-fat coconut milk, if you like) and the Cheddar cheese.

Per Serving
Calories: 597
Total fat: 47g
Protein: 29g
Total carbs: 20g
Fiber: 7g
Net carbs: 13g
Sodium: 433mg
Cholesterol: 155mg

Turkey Chili with Butternut Squash

Serves 6 • Prep: 15 minutes • Cook: 6 hours on low

Butternut squash adds a hint of sweetness, bright orange color, and tons of beta-carotene and other nutrients to this dish. The cinnamon is an unexpected flavor that pairs beautifully with the sweet squash and chili powder. Serve this chili with traditional chili toppings, or wrapped in a lettuce leaf "taco" or low-carb tortilla burrito.

¼ cup coconut oil, unsalted butter, or Ghee (page 179)

1¼ pounds ground turkey

1 onion, chopped

2 garlic cloves, minced

2 cups diced peeled butternut squash

2 cups chicken broth

1 (14.5-ounce) can diced tomatoes, with juice

2 tablespoons chili powder

1 teaspoon ground cumin

1 teaspoon ground cinnamon

1½ cups sour cream, divided

1½ cups shredded Cheddar cheese

2 avocados, peeled, pitted, and sliced

1. In a large skillet, heat the coconut oil over medium-high heat.

2. Add the turkey, onion, and garlic. Sauté until the turkey is browned and the onion is softened, about 4 minutes. Transfer to the slow cooker.

3. Stir in the squash, chicken broth, tomatoes and their juice, chili powder, cumin, and cinnamon. Cover and cook for 6 hours on low.

4. Just before serving, stir in ¾ cup of sour cream. Serve hot, garnished with the remaining ¾ cup of sour cream, Cheddar cheese, and avocado slices.

Variation Tip You can use ground beef instead of ground turkey if you like. Just be sure to use a slotted spoon to transfer the meat and onion mixture to the slow cooker, leaving behind the excess fat to avoid ending up with greasy chili.

Spicy Beef
& No-Bean Chili

Serves 8 • Prep: 15 minutes • Cook: 8 hours on low

QUICK PREP

MAKE IT
ALLERGEN-FREE

PALEO FRIENDLY

There is a never-ending debate about whether or not beans belong in chili, but one thing's for sure—they don't belong in a low-carb diet. This chili is so delicious, even if you are on the "real chili includes beans" side, you won't miss them here.

2½ pounds (70% lean) ground beef

2 teaspoons kosher salt

1 teaspoon freshly ground black pepper

1 red onion, diced, divided

6 garlic cloves, minced

3 celery stalks, diced

¼ cup sliced jalapeño peppers

1 (7-ounce) can diced fire-roasted green chiles, drained

1 (28-ounce) can diced tomatoes, with juice

1 (6-ounce) can tomato paste

3 tablespoons chili powder

3 tablespoons ground cumin

1 teaspoon dried oregano

1 bay leaf

Shredded Cheddar cheese, for garnish

Sour cream, for garnish

Sliced avocado, for garnish

Macronutrients
Fat 75%
Protein 17%
Carbs 8%

Per Serving
Calories: 685
Total fat: 58g
Protein: 28 g
Total carbs: 15g
Fiber: 5g
Net carbs: 10g
Sodium: 355mg
Cholesterol: 143mg

1. Heat a large skillet over medium-high heat. Add the beef, salt, and pepper and sauté until the beef is browned, about 5 minutes. Transfer to the slow cooker.

2. Stir in the onion, garlic, celery, jalapeños, green chiles, tomatoes and their juice, tomato paste, chili powder, cumin, oregano, and bay leaf. Cover and cook for 8 hours on low.

3. Discard the bay leaf and serve hot, garnished with Cheddar cheese, sour cream, and avocado.

Make It Allergen-Free/Paleo Simply omit the Cheddar and sour cream garnish.

FOUR

Vegetarian & Vegan Dishes

Macronutrients

Fat 73%

Protein 18%

Carbs 9%

Per Serving

Calories: 453

Total fat: 37g

Protein: 19g

Total carbs: 13g

Fiber: 2g

Net carbs: 11g

Sodium: 930mg

Cholesterol: 89mg

Mushroom Stroganoff

Serves 4 • Prep: 15 minutes • Cook: 6 hours on low

This hearty mushroom stew is ridiculously simple but full of rich flavor. Try this vegetarian stroganoff spooned over buttered zucchini noodles or spaghetti squash for a satisfying meal. Since this dish has no meat in it, and the sour cream isn't added until the end, it's a great candidate for being set up in the slow cooker in the morning with a delay timer set to start an hour or two after you leave for work.

¼ cup (½ stick) unsalted butter, cubed

1 pound cremini mushrooms, halved or quartered

1 large onion, halved and thinly sliced

4 garlic cloves, minced

2 cups Vegetable Broth (page 176)

4 teaspoons smoked paprika

½ teaspoon kosher salt

¼ teaspoon freshly ground black pepper

1½ cups sour cream

¼ cup chopped fresh flat-leaf parsley

1 cup grated Parmesan cheese

1. In the slow cooker, combine the butter, mushrooms, onion, garlic, vegetable broth, paprika, salt, and pepper. Cover and cook for 6 hours on low.

2. Just before serving, stir in the sour cream. Serve hot, garnished with the parsley and Parmesan cheese.

Make It Allergen-Free/Paleo Substitute coconut oil for the butter and full-fat plain cultured coconut yogurt for the sour cream, and omit the Parmesan cheese. Bonus: This also makes it vegan.

Cheesy Zucchini Lasagna

Serves 6 • Prep: 15 minutes • Cook: 7 hours on low or 3 ½ hours on high

QUICK PREP

FASTER COOK
OPTION

Layers of zucchini noodles sandwich saucy tomato sauce and three kinds of cheese for a decadent Italian meal. It's quick to prep and is just the kind of comfort food you want to come home to after a hard day at work.

Coconut oil, for coating the slow cooker insert

1 pound mascarpone cheese

1 cup grated Parmesan cheese, divided

1 cup chopped spinach

1 large egg, beaten

1 teaspoon dried oregano

¾ teaspoon kosher salt

½ teaspoon freshly ground black pepper

1½ cups tomato sauce, divided

1 cup heavy (whipping) cream

2 medium zucchini, cut into ⅓-inch slices

4 cups shredded fontina cheese

2 tablespoons chopped fresh flat-leaf parsley

Macronutrients

Fat 76%

Protein 20%

Carbs 4%

Per Serving

Calories: 696

Total fat: 61g

Protein: 31g

Total carbs: 8g

Fiber: 1g

Net carbs: 7g

Sodium: 905mg

Cholesterol: 231mg

1. Coat the inside of the slow cooker insert with coconut oil.

2. In a medium bowl, stir together the mascarpone cheese, ½ cup of Parmesan cheese, spinach, egg, oregano, salt, and pepper.

3. In a separate bowl, stir together the tomato sauce and heavy cream. Spoon 1 cup of the sauce into the slow cooker and spread it out to coat the bottom of the insert.

4. Arrange one-third of the zucchini slices in a single layer, or slightly overlapping, over the sauce.

5. Spread one-third of the mascarpone mixture over the zucchini slices, then top with one-third of the remaining tomato sauce, followed by one-third of the fontina cheese. Repeat the layers two more times.

6. Sprinkle the remaining ½ cup of Parmesan cheese over the top. Cover and cook for 7 hours on low or 3 ½ hours on high. Serve hot, garnished with the parsley.

Variation Tip If you have the time, turn off the slow cooker when the cooking time ends and let the lasagna sit for an additional 45 minutes before serving to allow some of the liquid released from the vegetables to be reabsorbed into the dish.

VEGETARIAN & VEGAN DISHES

Per Serving
Calories: 404
Total fat: 34g
Protein: 16g
Total carbs: 10g
Fiber: 2g
Net carbs: 8g
Sodium: 778mg
Cholesterol: 171mg

Cheese-Stuffed Peppers

Serves 6 • Prep: 15 minutes • Cook: 7 hours on low

Stuffed peppers are a classic comfort food. These don't take long to prep, but even so, you can do it all the night before. If you do, refrigerate the peppers overnight and put them in the slow cooker in the morning. It's a good idea to let them come to room temperature for about 30 minutes before turning on the slow cooker. If needed, set a delay timer to start 30 minutes after you leave. To prepare the riced cauliflower, trim off the root, chop the cauliflower into chunks, and pulse in a food processor until it is the texture of rice.

3 large bell peppers (any color), halved lengthwise, seeded, and ribbed

1 cup riced cauliflower

1 cup diced tomatoes

1 onion, diced

2 garlic cloves, minced

¼ cup (½ stick) unsalted butter or Ghee (page 179), melted

8 ounces cream cheese, cut into small pieces

2 cups shredded Cheddar cheese, divided

2 eggs, lightly beaten

1 teaspoon kosher salt

½ teaspoon freshly ground black pepper

1 cup Vegetable Broth (page 176)

1. Place the pepper halves in the slow cooker with the open sides up.

2. In a large bowl, mix together the cauliflower, tomatoes, onion, garlic, butter, cream cheese, 1½ cups of Cheddar cheese, eggs, salt, and pepper.

3. Spoon the cheese mixture into the peppers, dividing equally. Sprinkle the remaining ½ cup of Cheddar cheese over the top.

4. Pour the vegetable broth around the peppers. Cover and cook for 7 hours on low. Serve hot.

Variation Tip To brown the tops, once the cooking time is up, carefully transfer the peppers to a baking sheet and place under the broiler until the tops are bubbly and golden brown, 2 to 3 minutes.

Deep-Dish Cauliflower Crust Pizza with Olives

Serves 4 • Prep: 15 minutes • Cook: 6 hours on low or 3 hours on high

Macronutrients
Fat 70%
Protein 25%
Carbs 5%

Per Serving
Calories: 423
Total fat: 33g
Protein: 25g
Total carbs: 8g
Fiber: 2g
Net carbs: 6g
Sodium: 988mg
Cholesterol: 123mg

Pizza is one of the hardest things for me to give up when going low-carb. This version satisfies the urge, and it's super easy to make in the slow cooker. It uses three kinds of cheese for deep flavor—sharp Parmesan, melty fontina, and creamy mascarpone. To prepare the riced cauliflower, trim off the root, chop the cauliflower into chunks, and pulse in a food processor until it is the texture of rice.

3 cups riced cauliflower

3 cups shredded fontina cheese, divided

1 cup grated Parmesan cheese, divided

1 egg, lightly beaten

1 teaspoon dried Italian seasoning

¼ teaspoon kosher salt

Coconut oil, for coating the slow cooker insert

1 cup tomato sauce

4 ounces mascarpone cheese

1 cup Kalamata olives, pitted and halved

½ teaspoon dried rosemary

1. In a large bowl, stir together the cauliflower, 1 cup of fontina cheese, ½ cup of Parmesan cheese, egg, Italian seasoning, and salt. Mix well.

2. Coat the inside of the slow cooker insert with coconut oil and then press the cauliflower mixture into it in an even layer that is just slightly higher around the edges.

3. In a medium bowl, stir together the tomato sauce and mascarpone. Pour the mixture over the crust, spreading it into an even layer.

4. Top with the remaining 2 cups of fontina cheese and ½ cup of Parmesan cheese.

5. Sprinkle the olives and rosemary over the top. Put the lid on the slow cooker, but prop it slightly open with a chopstick or wooden spoon. Cook for 6 hours on low or 3 hours on high.

6. When finished, let the pizza sit in the slow cooker for 10 or 15 minutes more before serving. Serve warm.

Variation Tip Top this pizza with any number of vegetarian toppings. Different types of cheeses, fresh herbs, diced peppers, or chopped broccoli are all great options.

VEGETARIAN & VEGAN DISHES

Macronutrients
Fat 70%
Protein 20%
Carbs 10%

Per Serving
Calories: 350
Total fat: 29g
Protein: 16g
Total carbs: 11g
Fiber: 1g
Net carbs: 10g
Sodium: 767mg
Cholesterol: 0mg

Vegan Pumpkin Curry

Serves 4 • Prep: 15 minutes • Cook: 6 hours on low

This simple vegan curry is enriched with coconut milk. A topping of macadamia nuts adds enticing texture, delicious flavor, and also heart-healthy monounsaturated fat and omega-3 fatty acids, both of which help you lose weight. Macadamia nuts are also a rare source of palmitoleic acid, a monounsaturated fatty acid that may boost fat metabolism. Serve it over cauliflower rice cooked with coconut cream.

2 tablespoons coconut oil, melted

1½ pounds extra-firm tofu, cut into 1-inch cubes

12 ounces cremini or button mushrooms, halved or quartered

½ cup diced onion

2 garlic cloves, minced

1 tablespoon grated fresh ginger

3 tablespoons curry powder

1 teaspoon ground cumin

1 teaspoon kosher salt

½ teaspoon cayenne pepper

1 (14-ounce) can coconut milk

¼ cup chopped macadamia nuts

¼ cup chopped fresh cilantro

1. Coat the inside of the slow cooker insert with the coconut oil. Add the tofu, mushrooms, onion, garlic, ginger, curry powder, cumin, salt, cayenne, and coconut milk. Cover and cook for 6 hours on low.

2. Serve hot, garnished with the macadamia nuts and cilantro.

Variation Tip For even deeper flavor, before adding the ingredients to the slow cooker, sauté the onion and garlic in the coconut oil in a skillet over medium-high heat. Add the ginger, curry powder, cumin, salt, and cayenne and cook for 30 seconds longer. Transfer to the slow cooker, add the remaining ingredients, and proceed with the recipe as written.

Thai Green Curry
with Tofu & Vegetables

Serves 4 • Prep: 15 minutes • Cook: 7 hours on low

QUICK PREP

Macronutrients
Fat 70%
Protein 15%
Carbs 15%

Per Serving
Calories: 380
Total fat: 31g
Protein: 15g
Total carbs: 15g
Fiber: 6g
Net carbs: 9g
Sodium: 713mg
Cholesterol: 0mg

This Thai-style curry is a delicious, healthy meal for low-carb vegans. Tofu is a good keto-friendly protein since it is low in carbs (about 1 gram of net carbs per 4-ounce serving) and contains protein (10 grams per serving) and fat (5 grams per serving).

2 tablespoons coconut oil

½ onion, diced

1 tablespoon minced fresh ginger

2 garlic cloves, minced

1 pound firm tofu, diced

½ green bell pepper, seeded and sliced

1 (14-ounce) can coconut milk

¼ cup Thai green curry paste

1 tablespoon erythritol

1 teaspoon kosher salt

½ teaspoon turmeric

¼ cup chopped fresh cilantro, for garnish

1. In a medium skillet, heat the coconut oil over medium-high heat.

2. Add the onion and sauté until softened, about 5 minutes.

3. Stir in the ginger and garlic and then transfer the mixture to the slow cooker.

4. Mix in the tofu, green bell pepper, coconut milk, curry paste, erythritol, salt, and turmeric. Cover and cook for 7 hours on low. Serve hot, garnished with the cilantro.

Variation Tip To give the tofu a firmer texture, don't add it to the slow cooker initially. About 1 hour before the end of the cooking time, brown the tofu in coconut oil in a skillet over medium-high heat until golden on both sides. Then, 30 minutes before the end of the cooking time, add the tofu to the cooker, cover, and continue to cook.

Macronutrients
Fat 73%
Protein 23%
Carbs 4%

Per Serving
Calories: 355
Total fat: 29g
Protein: 20g
Total carbs: 6g
Fiber: 2g
Net carbs: 4g
Sodium: 1,487mg
Cholesterol: 51mg

Buffalo-Style Cauliflower Chili

Serves 4 • Prep: 10 minutes • Cook: 6 hours on low

This quick-prep vegetarian chili packs all the flavors of Buffalo wings in a healthy, low-carb, high-fat bowl of delicious. A topping of crumbled blue cheese and crunchy celery bits provides the full Buffalo wings experience.

2 tablespoons coconut oil

2 cups cauliflower florets

8 ounces firm tofu, cut into 1-inch cubes

½ onion, diced

2 cups crumbled blue cheese, divided

1 cup diced tomatoes, with juice

¼ cup all-natural spicy hot sauce (such as Frank's RedHot)

1 tablespoon erythritol

1½ teaspoons chili powder

1 teaspoon ground cumin

¼ teaspoon kosher salt

2 celery stalks, finely diced

1. In the slow cooker, combine the coconut oil, cauliflower, tofu, onion, 1 cup of blue cheese, tomatoes and their juice, hot sauce, erythritol, chili powder, cumin, and salt. Stir to mix. Cover and cook for 6 hours on low.

2. Serve the chili hot, topped with the celery and remaining 1 cup of blue cheese.

Variation Tip For added flavor and texture, brown the onion and tofu in the coconut oil in a skillet over medium-high heat before adding them to the slow cooker.

Vegan Green Bean & Mushroom Casserole

Serves 4 • Prep: 15 minutes • Cook: 6 hours on low or 3 hours on high

This hearty, creamy casserole evokes the traditional Thanksgiving dish, except this version is low-carb and vegan. The tofu gives it plenty of protein, so you can serve it as an entrée.

1 tablespoon coconut oil

½ onion, diced

6 ounces cremini or button mushrooms, sliced

2 garlic cloves, minced

2 teaspoons paprika

½ teaspoon kosher salt

¼ teaspoon freshly ground black pepper

½ cup Vegetable Broth (page 176)

1 pound firm tofu, cut into 1-inch cubes

1 cup chopped green beans

1 (14-ounce) can coconut milk

½ cup sliced almonds

Macronutrients
Fat 73%
Protein 17%
Carbs 10%

Per Serving
Calories: 383
Total fat: 31g
Protein: 15g
Total carbs: 11g
Fiber: 5g
Net carbs: 6g
Sodium: 684mg
Cholesterol: 0mg

1. In a large skillet, heat the coconut oil over medium-high heat.

2. Add the onion and sauté until it begins to soften, about 3 minutes.

3. Add the mushrooms and continue to sauté until softened, about 5 minutes more.

4. Stir in the garlic and sauté for about 30 seconds.

5. Stir in the paprika, salt, and pepper, and then add the vegetable broth to deglaze the skillet, scraping up any browned bits from the bottom. Transfer the mixture to the slow cooker.

6. Stir the tofu, green beans, and coconut milk into the cooker. Cover and cook for 6 hours on low or 3 hours on high. Serve hot, garnished with the almonds.

Variation Tip For a festive holiday-style dish, serve this casserole topped with crispy fried shallots or onions. Drop very thinly sliced shallots or onions into a saucepan of hot oil and fry over high heat for about 30 seconds until golden brown. Drain on paper towels and then crumble over the casserole.

VEGETARIAN & VEGAN DISHES

Macronutrients
Fat 70%
Protein 19%
Carbs 11%

Per Serving
Calories: 486
Total fat: 39g
Protein: 23g
Total carbs: 14g
Fiber: 3g
Net carbs: 11g
Sodium: 319mg
Cholesterol: 98mg

Spaghetti (Squash) with Creamy Tomato Sauce

Serves 4 • Prep: 10 minutes • Cook: 7 hours on low

If you're craving spaghetti, this rich, creamy, tomato-based sauce, enriched with melted cream cheese, made hearty with diced tofu, and spooned over tender spaghetti squash strands, is sure to satisfy. The best part of this dish is that the squash cooks right along with the sauce in the slow cooker.

1 tablespoon coconut oil

1 small spaghetti squash, halved, seeds and pulp removed

12 ounces firm tofu, finely diced

1 (14.5-ounce) can diced tomatoes

8 ounces cream cheese, at room temperature

½ onion, diced

4 garlic cloves, minced

1 teaspoon dried oregano

¾ teaspoon kosher salt

½ teaspoon freshly ground black pepper

2 tablespoons unsalted butter

1 cup grated Parmesan cheese, divided

1. Coat the bottom of the slow cooker insert with the coconut oil.

2. Place the spaghetti squash halves, cut-side down, in the bottom of the slow cooker insert.

3. In a large bowl, stir together the tofu, tomatoes, cream cheese, onion, garlic, oregano, salt, and pepper. Pour the mixture into the slow cooker, around the squash. Cover and cook for 7 hours on low.

4. Using tongs, carefully remove the spaghetti squash from the slow cooker. With a fork, shred the flesh into a colander. Let the strands drain for a few minutes and then transfer to a bowl and toss with the butter.

5. To serve, divide the squash among four serving plates, top with some tomato sauce, and garnish with the Parmesan cheese.

Variation Tip You can make the sauce without the spaghetti squash if you like. Serve the sauce over lightly steamed shredded cabbage, bean sprouts, or broccoli slaw instead.

Spinach & Cheese Stuffed Mushrooms with Fresh Thyme

Serves 6 • Prep: 15 minutes • Cook: 6 hours on low

QUICK PREP

Macronutrients
Fat 70%
Protein 21%
Carbs 9%

Per Serving
Calories: 382
Total fat: 31g
Protein: 20g
Total carbs: 9g
Fiber: 2g
Net carbs: 7g
Sodium: 366mg
Cholesterol: 115mg

Stuffed mushrooms are easy to make, but always feel a bit special. They strike that perfect balance between comfort food and party food. These are stuffed with a combination of chopped spinach and Gruyère cheese. Walnuts replace the usual bread crumbs and add a nice crunch to the filling.

2 tablespoons unsalted butter, Ghee (page 179), or extra-virgin olive oil

3 large eggs

2 cups shredded Gruyère cheese, divided

½ cup chopped walnuts, plus more for garnish

1½ pounds cremini or button mushrooms, stems minced, caps left whole

2 cups chopped spinach

½ onion, minced

2 garlic cloves, minced

1 tablespoon fresh thyme leaves, plus more for garnish

½ teaspoon kosher salt

½ teaspoon freshly ground black pepper

1. Generously coat the inside of the slow cooker insert with the butter.

2. In a medium bowl, beat the eggs, then stir in 1½ cups of Gruyère cheese, ½ cup of walnuts, the mushroom stems, spinach, onion, garlic, 1 tablespoon of thyme, salt, and pepper.

3. Spoon the mixture into the mushroom caps and place each filled cap in the bottom of the slow cooker in a single layer.

4. Sprinkle the remaining ½ cup of Gruyère cheese over the top. Cover and cook for 6 hours on low. Serve hot, garnished with additional thyme and chopped walnuts.

Variation Tip Instead of sprinkling the last ½ cup of Gruyère over the mushrooms before cooking, reserve the cheese. Cook the stuffed mushrooms for 6 hours. Transfer the mushrooms to a rimmed baking sheet and sprinkle the remaining Gruyère cheese and, if desired, ¼ cup finely chopped walnuts over the top. Broil until the cheese is melted and lightly browned, 2 to 3 minutes.

VEGETARIAN & VEGAN DISHES

QUICK PREP

FASTER COOK
OPTION

MAKE IT
ALLERGEN-FREE

PALEO FRIENDLY

Macronutrients

Fat 71%

Protein 16%

Carbs 13%

Per Serving
Calories: 354
Total fat: 28g
Protein: 20g
Total carbs: 12g
Fiber: 5g
Net carbs: 7g
Sodium: 503mg
Cholesterol: 46mg

Balsamic-Glazed Brussels Sprouts with Pine Nuts & Parmesan

Serves 6 • Prep: 10 minutes • Cook: 6 hours on low or 3 hours on high

Slow-cooked Brussels sprouts are deliciously tender. Add a balsamic glaze and a sprinkling of Parmesan cheese and pine nuts and this simple dish becomes a satisfying centerpiece for a vegetarian meal. It also makes a great side dish to roasted meats or other vegetarian entrées. Brussels sprouts are loaded with vitamin C, which helps the body absorb iron. This is especially helpful for vegetarians and vegans, who are at risk for iron deficiency.

1 pound Brussels sprouts, halved

2 tablespoons coconut oil

Kosher salt

Freshly ground black pepper

2 tablespoons unsalted butter, cubed

2 tablespoons balsamic vinegar

2 tablespoons erythritol

2 cups grated Parmesan cheese

¼ cup toasted pine nuts

1. In the slow cooker, combine the Brussels sprouts and coconut oil. Season with salt and pepper and stir to mix.

2. Top with the butter. Cover and cook for 6 hours on low or 3 hours on high.

3. In a small saucepan, combine the balsamic vinegar and erythritol over medium heat and bring to a boil. Reduce the heat a bit and simmer until the liquid is thick and syrupy, about 8 minutes.

4. To serve, drizzle the balsamic glaze over the Brussels sprouts and serve hot, garnished with the Parmesan cheese and pine nuts.

Make It Allergen-Free/Paleo Omit the Parmesan cheese and substitute coconut oil for the butter. You can substitute a combination of chopped macadamia nuts and nutritional yeast (for paleo) or sunflower seeds and nutritional yeast (for allergen-free). For paleo, substitute coconut sugar for the erythritol. Crispy fried onions or shallots would also make a good substitute or addition.

Crustless Quiche
with Spinach & Feta

Serves 6 • Prep: 10 minutes • Cook: 7 hours on low

Macronutrients
Fat 70%
Protein 25%
Carbs 5%

Per Serving
Calories: 856
Total fat: 67g
Protein: 58g
Total carbs: 7g
Fiber: 0g
Net carbs: 7g
Sodium: 899mg
Cholesterol:
1,806mg

Crustless quiche is a great vegetarian dinner option for low-carb dieters, and making it in the slow cooker makes it even more convenient. It's also incredibly versatile since it works equally well as a breakfast, brunch, lunch, or supper dish.

1 tablespoon unsalted butter or Ghee (page 179), at room temperature

10 large eggs

1 cup heavy (whipping) cream

2 cups spinach, chopped

¾ cup crumbled feta cheese

½ cup grated Parmesan cheese

2 garlic cloves, minced

½ teaspoon freshly ground black pepper

¼ teaspoon kosher salt

¼ cup grated sharp Cheddar cheese

1. Coat the inside of the slow cooker insert with the butter.

2. In the insert, whisk together the eggs and heavy cream.

3. Stir in the spinach, feta and Parmesan cheeses, garlic, pepper, and salt.

4. Sprinkle the Cheddar cheese over the top. Cover and cook for 7 hours on low. Serve hot, warm, or at room temperature.

Variation Tip This basic recipe can be jazzed up with any number of additional ingredients. Try adding chopped broccoli, fresh or roasted red bell peppers, olives, or minced fresh herbs.

VEGETARIAN & VEGAN DISHES

Per Serving
Calories: 536
Total fat: 43g
Protein: 29g
Total carbs: 13g
Fiber: 5g
Net carbs: 8g
Sodium: 746mg
Cholesterol: 87mg

Eggplant Parmesan

Serves 6 • Prep: 10 minutes • Cook: 8 hours on low or 4 hours on high

This simple layered eggplant Parmesan takes only minutes to put together and tastes amazing. The ground almond meal is a great stand-in for the traditional bread crumbs, providing crunch and a hint of toasty flavor. If you don't care for eggplant, substitute sliced zucchini or butternut squash.

2 tablespoons coconut oil

2 cups tomato sauce

8 ounces mascarpone cheese

8 ounces eggplant, peeled and thinly sliced

3 cups shredded fontina cheese

1 cup grated Parmesan cheese

1 cup coarsely ground almond meal

1. Coat the inside of the slow cooker insert with the coconut oil.

2. In a medium bowl, stir together the tomato sauce and mascarpone. Coat the bottom of the insert with ½ cup of sauce.

3. Arrange several eggplant slices in a single layer, or slightly overlapping, over the sauce.

4. Top with a bit of fontina cheese, a bit of Parmesan cheese, a sprinkling of almond meal, and more sauce. Continue layering until you've used all the ingredients, ending with a layer of sauce, then cheese, and then almond meal. Cover and cook for 8 hours on low or 4 hours on high. Serve hot.

Variation Tip Salting the eggplant and letting the salt draw out the excess moisture before creating your layers makes this great dish even better. Arrange the eggplant slices on a clean kitchen towel and sprinkle with a generous amount of salt. Let sit for 1 to 2 hours. Rinse the slices under cold water and then pat dry before creating your layers in the slow cooker. This process pulls excess moisture from the vegetable, giving it a superior texture after it is cooked.

Slow Cooker Enchilada Casserole

Serves 6 • Prep: 15 minutes • Cook: 6 hours on low or 3 hours on high

Who needs tortillas? Strips of canned roasted mild green chiles separate the layers of this cheesy, saucy casserole. Try making homemade Enchilada Sauce (page 180), or use 3 cups of a purchased variety, but check the ingredients for high-carb offenders, such as starchy thickeners, preservatives, and other artificial additives.

1 tablespoon coconut oil

4 large eggs

2 cups sour cream

12 ounces cream cheese, at room temperature

1½ cups grated sharp Cheddar cheese, divided

1 cup heavy (whipping) cream

1 teaspoon dried oregano

1 teaspoon kosher salt

2 (7-ounce) cans whole roasted green chiles, drained and seeded

1 pound frozen spinach, thawed

1 recipe Enchilada Sauce (page 180)

¼ cup chopped fresh cilantro

4 scallions, sliced

Macronutrients
Fat 79%
Protein 16%
Carbs 5%

Per Serving
Calories: 865
Total fat: 77g
Protein: 36g
Total carbs: 12g
Fiber: 2g
Net carbs: 10g
Sodium: 1,235mg
Cholesterol: 871mg

1. Coat the inside of the slow cooker insert with the coconut oil.

2. In a large bowl, beat the eggs, then whisk in the sour cream, cream cheese, 1 cup of Cheddar cheese, heavy cream, oregano, and salt.

3. Lay several strips of green chiles in a single layer on the bottom of the slow cooker to cover it.

4. Dollop one-third of the cheese mixture on top, distributing it evenly. Spread it out with the back of the spoon.

5. Top with one-third of the spinach, and then 1 cup of enchilada sauce. Repeat twice more with the remaining ingredients.

6. Sprinkle the remaining ½ cup of Cheddar cheese over the top layer. Cover and cook for 6 hours on low or 3 hours on high. Serve hot, garnished with the cilantro and scallions.

Variation Tip Substitute low-carb flour tortillas for the green chiles or make your own grain-free version: whisk 2 eggs, 1 teaspoon melted coconut oil, 1 tablespoon water, ¼ cup arrowroot powder, 1 teaspoon almond flour, and a pinch salt. Scoop ¼ cup of batter into a skillet set over medium heat and cook for 1 minute per side. Repeat with the remaining batter.

VEGETARIAN & VEGAN DISHES

Macronutrients

Fat 74%

Protein 13%

Carbs 13%

Per Serving

Calories: 367

Total fat: 34g

Protein: 13g

Total carbs: 14g

Fiber: 5g

Net carbs: 9g

Sodium: 18mg

Cholesterol: 0mg

Mushroom No-Meatballs in Tomato Sauce

Serves 4 • Prep: 15 minutes • Cook: 6 hours on low or 3 hours on high

These vegan no-meatballs are surprisingly filling. Made with protein-packed walnuts and flavorful mushrooms, they are as satisfying as any meat-filled version. Serve these over zucchini noodles or spaghetti squash, and add a sprinkling of grated Parmesan cheese if you eat dairy, or a sprinkling of nutritional yeast if you don't.

2 tablespoons coconut oil, plus more for coating the slow cooker insert

½ onion, diced

1 garlic clove, minced

1½ cups raw walnuts

10 ounces mushrooms, roughly chopped

2 tablespoons almond flour

1½ teaspoons dried basil

1 teaspoon dried oregano

¾ teaspoon kosher salt

1½ cups tomato sauce

1. Coat the inside of the slow cooker insert with coconut oil.

2. In a large skillet, heat 2 tablespoons of coconut oil over medium-high heat. Add the onion and garlic and sauté until softened, about 5 minutes.

3. Meanwhile, in a food processor, combine the walnuts, mushrooms, almond flour, basil, oregano, and salt. Pulse until everything is minced and well combined.

4. Add the cooked onion and garlic and pulse again until combined.

5. Form the nut mixture into 1½-inch balls and place them in the slow cooker.

6. Pour the tomato sauce over the top. Cover and cook for 6 hours on low or 3 hours on high. Serve hot.

Variation Tip For added flavor, before adding to the slow cooker, brown the no-meatballs briefly in hot coconut oil in a skillet, cooking for about 2 minutes per side until nicely browned.

Fennel & Cauliflower Gratin

Serves 6 • Prep: 10 minutes • Cook: 6 hours on low or 3 hours on high

I think fennel is one of the most underutilized vegetables. It's full of flavor and is delicious raw or cooked. Here, it is topped with three kinds of cheese and slow cooked, along with cauliflower, until very tender. This makes a lovely vegetarian main dish for a special meal.

Coconut oil, unsalted butter, or Ghee (page 179), for coating the slow cooker insert

2 cups sliced fennel

2 cups cauliflower florets

1 onion, halved and sliced

2 garlic cloves, minced

2 cups shredded Gruyère cheese, divided

8 ounces cream cheese, at room temperature

Kosher salt

Freshly ground black pepper

½ cup freshly grated Parmesan cheese

½ cup almond meal

Macronutrients
Fat 73%
Protein 20%
Carbs 7%

Per Serving
Calories: 410
Total fat: 33g
Protein: 20g
Total carbs: 9g
Fiber: 3g
Net carbs: 6g
Sodium: 380mg
Cholesterol: 90mg

1. Generously coat the inside of the slow cooker insert with coconut oil.

2. In the slow cooker, combine the fennel, cauliflower, onion, and garlic. Toss to mix.

3. Stir in 1 cup of Gruyère cheese and the cream cheese. Season with salt and pepper.

4. Sprinkle the remaining 1 cup of Gruyère over the top.

5. Sprinkle the Parmesan cheese and almond meal over the Gruyère. Cover and cook for 6 hours on low or 3 hours on high. Serve hot.

Variation Tip For a crisper topping, don't sprinkle the remaining Gruyère, Parmesan, and almond meal over the top before cooking. At the end of the cooking time, transfer the vegetable mixture from the slow cooker to a baking dish, spreading it out in an even layer. Sprinkle the remaining 1 cup of Gruyère, the Parmesan, and the almond meal over that and broil until the cheese is melted and bubbly and the topping is golden brown, 3 to 5 minutes.

Macronutrients
Fat 70%
Protein 19%
Carbs 11%

Per Serving
Calories: 416
Total fat: 32g
Protein: 21g
Total carbs: 13g
Fiber: 2g
Net carbs: 11g
Sodium: 700mg
Cholesterol: 71mg

Squash Boats Filled with Spinach-Artichoke Gratin

Serves 4 • Prep: 10 minutes • Cook: 6 hours on low or 3 hours on high

Remember that delicious cheesy spinach and artichoke dip you loved scooping up with hunks of crusty bread at parties? Well, here it's cooked inside edible bowls of delicata squash. So satisfying and delicious, you definitely won't miss the bread.

1 tablespoon coconut oil

1½ cups grated Parmesan cheese, divided

½ cup sour cream

¼ cup mayonnaise

½ onion, diced

3 garlic cloves, minced

Kosher salt

Freshly ground black pepper

1 cup chopped baby spinach

½ cup chopped artichoke hearts

2 small delicata squashs, halved lengthwise and seeded

1 cup shredded fontina cheese

1 tablespoon chopped fresh flat-leaf parsley

1. Coat the inside of the slow cooker insert with the coconut oil.

2. In a medium bowl, stir together ¾ cup of Parmesan cheese, sour cream, mayonnaise, onion, and garlic until well combined. Season with salt and pepper.

3. Add the spinach and artichoke hearts and stir gently to mix.

4. Spoon the mixture into the squash halves, dividing evenly. Place the filled halves in the slow cooker in a single layer. Sprinkle the fontina cheese and remaining ¾ cup of Parmesan over the top. Cover and cook for 6 hours on low or 3 hours on high. Serve hot, garnished with the parsley.

Variation Tip To brown the topping, transfer the cooked squash from the slow cooker to a baking dish. Heat under the broiler until the cheese is bubbly and browned, 2 to 3 minutes.

Vegetarian Mole Chili

Serves 8 • Prep: 15 minutes • Cook: 8 hours on low or 4 hours on high

This chili recipe contains a surprise ingredient: cocoa powder. It balances the kick of the chili powder and jalapeño peppers and, along with the cinnamon, adds deep, earthy flavor. Serve this chili with the usual chili fixins—sour cream, shredded Cheddar cheese, and guacamole or sliced avocado.

Macronutrients
Fat 78%
Protein 15%
Carbs 7%

¼ cup coconut oil

1 pound firm tofu, diced

1 (14.5-ounce) can diced tomatoes, with juice

1 onion, diced

3 garlic cloves, minced

1 or 2 jalapeño peppers, seeded and minced

3 tablespoons unsweetened cocoa powder

2 tablespoons chili powder

1½ teaspoons paprika

1½ teaspoons ground cumin

1 teaspoon ground cinnamon

1 teaspoon kosher salt

½ teaspoon dried oregano

2½ cups sour cream, divided

2 cups shredded Cheddar cheese

1 avocado, peeled, pitted, and sliced

Per Serving
Calories: 392
Total fat: 34g
Protein: 15g
Total carbs: 9g
Fiber: 2g
Net carbs: 7g
Sodium: 519mg
Cholesterol: 61mg

1. In the slow cooker, combine the coconut oil, tofu, tomatoes and their juice, onion, garlic, jalapeños, cocoa powder, chili powder, paprika, cumin, cinnamon, salt, and oregano. Cover and cook for 8 hours on low or 4 hours on high.

2. Just before serving, stir in 1½ cups of sour cream. Serve hot, garnished with the remaining 1 cup of sour cream, Cheddar cheese, and avocado.

Variation Tip To give the tofu a firmer texture, 30 minutes before cooking, slice it into 1-inch-thick slabs. Line a rimmed baking sheet with a double layer of paper towels and arrange the tofu on top in a single layer. Top with another double layer of paper towels and then another baking sheet weighed down with a few heavy items, such as jars or books. Let sit for 30 minutes to release excess liquid. Pour off any released liquid, dice the tofu, and proceed with the recipe as written.

FIVE
Poultry & Pork Dishes

Macronutrients
Fat 73%
Protein 22%
Carbs 5%

Per Serving
Calories: 495
Total fat: 41g
Protein: 26g
Total carbs: 6g
Fiber: 1g
Net carbs: 5g
Sodium: 912mg
Cholesterol: 163mg

Creamy Garlic-Parmesan Chicken

Serves 8 • Prep: 15 minutes • Cook: 6 hours on low

I wanted to start this chapter with this incredibly simple recipe both because it makes for a delicious, low-carb dinner and because it's a great, easy way to cook a bunch of chicken to use in other dishes. You can layer it in an enchilada casserole or toss it with zucchini noodles. The sauce is cheesy, creamy, and divine.

2 pounds boneless, skinless chicken thighs

½ cup (1 stick) unsalted butter, melted

12 ounces cremini or button mushrooms, halved or quartered

1 onion, diced

8 garlic cloves, minced

2 teaspoons paprika

2 teaspoons kosher salt

1 teaspoon freshly ground black pepper

1 cup chicken broth

8 ounces cream cheese

1 cup grated Parmesan cheese

Fresh parsley, for garnish

1. Put the chicken pieces in the slow cooker. Pour the melted butter over the chicken. Add the mushrooms, onion, garlic, paprika, salt, and pepper and toss to coat the chicken with the butter. Cover and cook for 6 hours on low.

2. When finished, transfer the chicken and vegetables to a serving platter.

3. In a saucepan over medium heat, combine the chicken broth, cream cheese, and Parmesan cheese. Cook, stirring, until the cream cheese is melted and fully incorporated, about 5 minutes. Pour the sauce over the chicken and serve, garnished with parsley.

Make It Allergen-Free/Paleo Use coconut oil in place of the butter, substitute 1½ cups coconut cream for the cream cheese, and omit the Parmesan cheese.

Pulled Chicken with Low-Carb Barbecue Sauce

Serves 6 • Prep: 10 minutes • Cook: 8 hours on low

QUICK PREP

MAKE IT
ALLERGEN-FREE

PALEO FRIENDLY

Most barbecue sauces are loaded with sugar or other high-carb sweeteners. This one uses the natural, low-carb sweetener erythritol. The result is a tangy-sweet-spicy barbecue sauce that is low in carbs but full of flavor. Serve this alongside garlicky sautéed greens to get your barbecue fix.

4 bacon slices, diced

½ cup (1 stick) unsalted butter, melted

¼ cup red wine vinegar

¼ cup chicken broth

¼ cup tomato paste

¼ cup prepared mustard

1 tablespoon soy sauce or tamari

1 teaspoon fish sauce or additional soy sauce or tamari

¼ cup erythritol

2 teaspoons chili powder

1 teaspoon ground cumin

1 teaspoon cayenne pepper

1½ pounds boneless, skinless chicken thighs

1. In a skillet, cook the bacon over medium-high heat until browned and crisp, about 5 minutes. Transfer it, along with the rendered bacon fat, to the slow cooker.

2. Stir in the butter, red wine vinegar, chicken broth, tomato paste, mustard, soy sauce, fish sauce, erythritol, chili powder, cumin, and cayenne.

3. Add the chicken to the sauce and stir to coat. Cover and cook for 8 hours on low.

4. Transfer the chicken to a bowl or work surface. Using two forks, shred the chicken and then return the shredded meat to the sauce. Serve hot.

Make It Allergen-Free/Paleo To make this paleo, substitute Ghee (page 179) or coconut oil for the butter, fish sauce for the soy sauce, and coconut sugar for the erythritol. To make it allergen-free, use coconut oil in place of the butter and coconut aminos in place of the soy sauce and fish sauce.

Macronutrients
Fat 77%
Protein 20%
Carbs 3%

Per Serving
Calories: 484
Total fat: 42g
Protein: 23g
Total carbs: 3g
Fiber: 1g
Net carbs: 2g
Sodium: 513mg
Cholesterol: 149mg

POULTRY & PORK DISHES

Macronutrients
Fat 76%
Protein 20%
Carbs 4%

Per Serving
Calories: 477
Total fat: 42g
Protein: 22g
Total carbs: 5g
Fiber: 1g
Net carbs: 4g
Sodium: 106mg
Cholesterol: 116mg

Indian Butter Chicken

Serves 6 • Prep: 10 minutes • Cook: 7 hours on low

Succulent chicken pieces are bathed in a creamy tomato sauce flavored with Indian spices and fresh ginger. To make morning prep easier, make the sauce the night before and refrigerate it. In the morning, transfer the sauce to the slow cooker, add the chicken, and you're good to go. Serve this spicy chicken over cauliflower rice.

1¼ cups coconut cream

1 cup tomato sauce

¼ cup (½ stick) unsalted butter, melted

2 teaspoons freshly squeezed lemon juice

4 garlic cloves, minced

2 shallots, finely diced

1 tablespoon minced fresh ginger

2 teaspoons garam masala

1 teaspoon chili powder

1 teaspoon ground cumin

¾ teaspoon cayenne pepper

1 bay leaf

Kosher salt

Freshly ground black pepper

1½ pounds boneless, skinless chicken thighs, cubed

1. In the slow cooker, stir together the coconut cream, tomato sauce, butter, lemon juice, garlic, shallots, ginger, garam masala, chili powder, cumin, cayenne, and bay leaf. Season with salt and pepper.

2. Add the chicken and toss to mix. Cover and cook for 7 hours on low. Discard the bay leaf and serve hot.

Make It Allergen-Free/Paleo Substitute coconut oil for the butter.

Chicken in Mushroom-Bacon Cream

Serves 6 • Prep: 15 minutes • Cook: 6 hours on low or 3 hours on high

This simple chicken preparation makes a perfect weeknight meal or centerpiece for a Sunday dinner. Serve it with roasted Brussels sprouts sprinkled with grated Parmesan cheese or a crisp green salad with a balsamic vinegar and olive oil dressing.

8 ounces bacon, diced

1½ pounds boneless, skinless chicken thighs

½ cup dry white wine

¼ cup (½ stick) unsalted butter, cubed

8 ounces cremini or button mushrooms, halved or quartered

1 onion, diced

6 garlic cloves, minced

3 fresh rosemary sprigs

1 teaspoon kosher salt

1 cup sour cream

Macronutrients
Fat 77%
Protein 20%
Carbs 3%

Per Serving
Calories: 570
Total fat: 49g
Protein: 27g
Total carbs: 5g
Fiber: 1g
Net carbs: 4g
Sodium: 433mg
Cholesterol: 161mg

1. In a large skillet, cook the bacon over medium-high heat until crisp, about 5 minutes. Transfer the bacon to the slow cooker.

2. Return the skillet to medium-high heat and add the chicken. Sauté until browned on both sides, about 4 minutes. Transfer the chicken to the slow cooker.

3. Add the wine to the skillet and bring to a boil. Cook for about 1 minute, stirring and scraping up any browned bits stuck to the bottom of the pan. Transfer to the slow cooker.

4. Add the butter, mushrooms, onion, garlic, rosemary, and salt to the slow cooker. Cover and cook for 6 hours on low or 3 hours on high.

5. Remove the chicken pieces and vegetables from the slow cooker and arrange them on a serving platter. Discard the rosemary sprigs. Stir the sour cream into the sauce in the cooker until well incorporated. Ladle the sauce over the chicken on the platter and serve hot.

Make It Allergen-Free/Paleo Substitute chicken or vegetable broth for the wine, coconut cream for the sour cream, and coconut oil for the butter.

POULTRY & PORK DISHES

QUICK PREP

FASTER COOK
OPTION

MAKE IT
ALLERGEN-FREE

PALEO FRIENDLY

Macronutrients
Fat 73%
Protein 20%
Carbs 7%

Per Serving
Calories: 692
Total fat: 58g
Protein: 33g
Total carbs: 14g
Fiber: 7g
Net carbs: 7g
Sodium: 553mg
Cholesterol: 175mg

Low-Carb Chicken Tacos

Serves 6 · Prep: 10 minutes · Cook: 6 hours on low or 3 hours on high

Cutting down on carbs is one thing, but cutting out taco night? Unacceptable. This recipe is so easy and produces such a delicious spicy, saucy shredded chicken filling that you won't even miss the tortillas. Use a type of lettuce with large, crisp leaves, such as iceberg, and top with the usual taco fixins—shredded cheese, sour cream, avocado slices, and hot sauce, if you like—and you'll be in taco heaven.

¼ cup (½ stick) unsalted butter, melted

1 cup diced tomatoes

1 cup halved green olives

½ onion, diced

2 garlic cloves, minced

1 or 2 jalapeño peppers, seeded and minced

1½ tablespoons chili powder

1½ teaspoons ground cumin

1 teaspoon dried oregano

1 teaspoon paprika

½ teaspoon kosher salt

¼ teaspoon freshly ground black pepper

1½ pounds boneless, skinless chicken thighs

1 cup sour cream

12 large lettuce leaves

2 cups shredded Cheddar cheese

2 avocados, peeled, pitted, and sliced

1. In the slow cooker, stir together the butter, tomatoes, olives, onion, garlic, jalapeños, chili powder, cumin, oregano, paprika, salt, and pepper.

2. Place the chicken pieces in the cooker and stir to coat them in the sauce. Cover and cook for 6 hours on low or 3 hours on high.

3. Transfer the chicken pieces to a bowl or work surface. Using two forks, shred the chicken and then return the shredded meat to the slow cooker.

4. Stir in the sour cream.

5. To serve, spoon the chicken mixture into the lettuce leaves and garnish with Cheddar cheese and avocado slices.

Make It Allergen-Free/Paleo Substitute coconut oil for the butter, coconut cream or cashew cream for the sour cream, and cashew cheese for the Cheddar cheese.

Mandarin Orange Chicken

Serves 6 • Prep: 10 minutes • Cook: 6 hours on low

QUICK PREP

Mandarin orange chicken is a takeout favorite, but the restaurant version is usually loaded with sugar and carbs. Using fresh oranges and substituting erythritol for the sugar makes this version keto friendly. Best of all, it has all the sweet, spicy, tangy flavor you crave.

1½ pounds bone-in, skin-on chicken thighs

1 tablespoon Chinese five-spice powder

½ teaspoon kosher salt

6 bacon slices, diced

1 large orange, sliced

1 small red chile pepper, very thinly sliced, or ½ teaspoon red pepper flakes

1 garlic clove, minced

1 tablespoon minced fresh ginger

¼ cup Asian sesame paste

2 tablespoons soy sauce or tamari

1 tablespoon freshly squeezed lime juice

1 tablespoon toasted sesame oil

1 tablespoon erythritol

¼ cup (½ stick) unsalted butter, cubed

½ cup chopped macadamia nuts

1. Season the chicken thighs all over with the five-spice powder and salt. Set aside.

2. In a large skillet, cook the bacon over medium-high heat until crisp and browned, about 5 minutes. Transfer the bacon to the slow cooker.

3. To the slow cooker, add the orange slices, red chile pepper, garlic, ginger, sesame paste, soy sauce, lime juice, sesame oil, and erythritol. Stir to mix.

4. Return the skillet to medium-high heat and add the seasoned chicken, skin-side down. Cook until browned, about 3 minutes per side. Arrange the browned chicken in the slow cooker, skin-side up. Top with the butter pieces. Cover and cook for 6 hours on low. Serve hot, garnished with the macadamia nuts.

Variation Tip For a thicker sauce, transfer the chicken and orange slices from the slow cooker to a serving platter. Pour the sauce into a blender (or use an immersion blender directly in the cooker), add ½ teaspoon of xanthan gum, and blend well. Pour the sauce over the chicken.

Macronutrients
Fat 76%
Protein 18%
Carbs 6%

Per Serving
Calories: 641
Total fat: 56g
Protein: 27g
Total carbs: 10g
Fiber: 3g
Net carbs: 7g
Sodium: 1,043mg
Cholesterol: 135mg

POULTRY & PORK DISHES

Macronutrients
Fat 75%
Protein 20%
Carbs 5%

Per Serving
Calories: 471
Total fat: 40g
Protein: 23g
Total carbs: 6g
Fiber: 1g
Net carbs: 5g
Sodium: 543mg
Cholesterol: 155mg

Chicken Paprikash

Serves 6 • Prep: 10 minutes • Cook: 8 hours on low

This hearty chicken stew has just a few ingredients but tons of flavor thanks to sweet Hungarian paprika, onions, garlic, and a bit of tomato paste. Sour cream is stirred in after cooking, adding richness and thickening the sauce. Serve this ladled over zucchini noodles or spaghetti squash.

½ onion, thinly sliced

1½ pounds boneless, skinless chicken thighs

1 teaspoon kosher salt

½ teaspoon freshly ground black pepper

3 tablespoons sweet Hungarian paprika

8 ounces cremini or button mushrooms, sliced

¼ cup (½ stick) unsalted butter, melted

½ cup chicken broth or water

2 tablespoons tomato paste

1 garlic clove, minced

⅓ teaspoon cayenne pepper

2 cups sour cream

1. Cover the bottom of the slow cooker with the onion slices.

2. Season the chicken pieces all over with the salt, pepper, and paprika. Arrange the chicken on top of the onions.

3. Scatter the mushrooms over the chicken and drizzle the melted butter over the top.

4. In a small bowl, whisk together the chicken broth, tomato paste, garlic, and cayenne. Pour this sauce over the chicken. Cover and cook for 8 hours on low.

5. Transfer the chicken pieces to a bowl and shred the meat using two forks.

6. Stir the sour cream into the sauce in the slow cooker until well incorporated. Return the chicken meat to the slow cooker and stir to mix. Serve hot.

Make It Allergen-Free/Paleo Substitute coconut oil for the butter and cashew cream for the sour cream.

Caribbean-Style Jerk Chicken

Serves 8 • Prep: 30 minutes • Cook: 6 hours on low

This flavorful chicken cooks in an island-style sauce of ginger, chiles, coconut milk, lime juice, and spices. Serve with cauliflower rice or use it as a filling for lettuce wraps.

1 (14-ounce) can coconut milk

¼ cup coconut oil

Juice of 1 lime

2 tablespoons blackstrap molasses

8 scallions, coarsely chopped

3 garlic cloves, peeled

2 habanero peppers, halved and seeded

1 (1-inch) fresh ginger, peeled and roughly chopped

1 tablespoon fresh thyme

2 teaspoons ground allspice

1 teaspoon kosher salt

¼ teaspoon ground cardamom

2 pounds boneless, skinless chicken thighs

Lime wedges, for garnish

Macronutrients
Fat 73%
Protein 21%
Carbs 6%

Per Serving
Calories: 413
Total fat: 35g
Protein: 21g
Total carbs: 6g
Fiber: 0g
Net carbs: 6g
Sodium: 386mg
Cholesterol: 95mg

1. In a food processor or blender, combine the coconut milk, coconut oil, lime juice, molasses, scallions, garlic, habaneros, ginger, thyme, allspice, salt, and cardamom. Process to combine well.

2. Put the chicken in the slow cooker and pour in the sauce. Toss to coat the chicken evenly with the sauce. Cover and cook for 6 hours on low. Serve hot, garnished with lime wedges.

Variation Tip If you have time before serving the chicken, leave the coconut milk and lime juice out of the blended seasoning mixture and use bone-in, skin-on chicken thighs. Cook the chicken per the recipe with the seasoning mixture. When finished, place an oiled rack on a baking sheet and transfer the chicken to the rack, skin-side down. Broil until browned and crisp, about 5 minutes per side. Meanwhile, stir the coconut milk and lime juice into the juices in the slow cooker. Place the browned chicken on a serving platter, pour the sauce over the top, and serve hot.

Macronutrients
Fat 77%
Protein 19%
Carbs 4%

Per Serving
Calories: 378
Total fat: 33g
Protein: 16g
Total carbs: 4g
Fiber: 1g
Net carbs: 3g
Sodium: 784mg
Cholesterol: 88mg

Bacon-Wrapped Chicken with Barbecue Sauce

Serves 4 • Prep: 15 minutes • Cook: 8 hours on low

When you start to get bored of chicken, just wrap it in bacon and douse it with tangy-sweet-spicy barbecue sauce. You'll fall in love all over again. This is a great family-friendly recipe. I mean, really, who doesn't love bacon? And barbecue sauce? Nobody, that's who.

12 bacon slices

4 large boneless, skinless chicken thighs

3 tablespoons red wine vinegar

3 tablespoons chicken broth

3 tablespoons tomato paste

3 tablespoons prepared mustard

2 tablespoons unsalted butter, melted

2 teaspoons soy sauce or tamari

1 teaspoon fish sauce or additional soy sauce or tamari

3 tablespoons erythritol or ¼ teaspoon stevia powder

2 teaspoons chili powder

1 teaspoon ground cumin

½ teaspoon cayenne pepper

½ onion, diced

1. Wrap 3 pieces of bacon around each chicken thigh. Place the wrapped chicken in the slow cooker in a single layer.

2. In a medium bowl, whisk together the red wine vinegar, chicken broth, tomato paste, mustard, butter, soy sauce, fish sauce, erythritol, chili powder, cumin, and cayenne. Stir in the onion. Pour the mixture over the chicken. Cover and cook for 8 hours on low. Serve hot.

Make It Allergen-Free/Paleo To make this paleo, substitute Ghee (page 179) or coconut oil for the butter and use fish sauce in place of the soy sauce. To make it allergen-free, use coconut oil in place of the butter and coconut aminos in place of the soy sauce and fish sauce.

Fontina-Stuffed Turkey Meatballs in Sauce

Serves 8 • Prep: 20 minutes • Cook: 7 hours on low

PALEO FRIENDLY

WORTH THE EFFORT

Ground turkey is a great source of protein because it is economical and a cinch to cook. Because of its mild flavor, it takes well to many different preparations. Here, it is flavored with Italian seasonings, formed into balls, stuffed with an ooey-gooey, melty cheese, and then cooked in a garlicky marinara-style sauce. For a "spaghetti and meatballs" experience, serve this over spaghetti squash or zucchini noodles. To prepare the riced cauliflower, trim off the root, chop the cauliflower into chunks, and pulse in a food processor until it is the texture of rice.

FOR THE SAUCE

¼ cup (½ stick) unsalted butter, melted

1 (14.5-ounce) can crushed tomatoes

1 tablespoon extra-virgin olive oil

2 garlic cloves, minced

2 teaspoons dried basil

1 teaspoon dried parsley

1 teaspoon kosher salt

½ teaspoon freshly ground black pepper

1 cup heavy (whipping) cream

TO MAKE THE SAUCE

In the slow cooker, stir together the butter, tomatoes, olive oil, garlic, basil, parsley, salt, and pepper.

→

Macronutrients
Fat 71%
Protein 24%
Carbs 5%

Per Serving
Calories: 633
Total fat: 50g
Protein: 39g
Total carbs: 9g
Fiber: 3g
Net carbs: 6g
Sodium: 1,529mg
Cholesterol: 208mg

POULTRY & PORK DISHES

FOR THE MEATBALLS

2 large eggs

2 cups riced cauliflower

½ cup almond meal

2 cups grated Parmesan cheese, divided

2 tablespoons Italian seasoning

1 teaspoon kosher salt

½ teaspoon freshly ground black pepper

½ teaspoon garlic powder

12 ounces ground turkey

1 pound Italian sausage, casings removed

8 ounces fontina cheese, cut into 24 cubes

TO MAKE THE MEATBALLS

1. In a large bowl, beat the eggs, then whisk in the cauliflower rice, almond meal, 1 cup of Parmesan cheese, Italian seasoning, salt, pepper, and garlic powder.

2. Add the turkey and sausage and mix to combine. Form the mixture into 24 (1-inch) balls.

3. Stuff a cheese cube into the center of each meatball and press the meat mixture around it so it is fully encased. Place the stuffed meatballs in the slow cooker. Cover and cook for 7 hours on low.

4. Just before serving, stir the heavy cream into the sauce. Serve hot, garnished with the remaining 1 cup of Parmesan cheese.

Make It Paleo Omit the fontina cheese, the Parmesan cheese, and the heavy cream and double the quantity of almond meal. To replace the heavy cream, use a nondairy substitute or make cashew cream: Soak 1 cup raw cashews in water for 3 hours. Drain, then process in a blender with ¾ cup water, 2 tablespoons freshly squeezed lemon juice, and ½ teaspoon kosher salt.

Turkish-Spiced Turkey Meatballs with Yogurt-Tahini Sauce

Serves 6 • Prep: 15 minutes • Cook: 7 hours on low

QUICK PREP
PALEO FRIENDLY

Macronutrients
Fat 68%
Protein 24%
Carbs 8%

Per Serving
Calories: 443
Total fat: 35g
Protein: 25g
Total carbs: 9g
Fiber: 1g
Net carbs: 8g
Sodium: 1,227mg
Cholesterol: 113mg

These turkey meatballs are similar to kofta and other Middle Eastern ground meat dishes usually made with lamb or beef. Here they're flavored with mint, feta cheese, and Middle Eastern spices. A rich yogurt sauce gets depth of flavor from tahini. Sumac is a bright red berry that is dried and ground and used as a seasoning in many Middle Eastern cuisines. It has a bright, tangy flavor. Za'atar is a spice mixture that includes sumac as well as dried thyme and sesame seeds. Serve these meatballs and sauce with a mixed green salad.

FOR THE MEATBALLS

1¼ pounds ground turkey

1 cup crumbled feta cheese

½ cup finely chopped walnuts

½ cup minced fresh mint

¼ cup grated onion

4 garlic cloves, minced

3 tablespoons paprika

1 tablespoon ground cumin

1½ teaspoons kosher salt

1 teaspoon freshly ground black pepper

¼ to ½ teaspoon cayenne pepper

2 tablespoons extra-virgin olive oil

1 onion, halved and thinly sliced

1 cup chicken broth

TO MAKE THE MEATBALLS

1. In a large bowl, stir together the ground turkey, feta, walnuts, mint, onion, garlic, paprika, cumin, salt, black pepper, and cayenne pepper. Form the mixture into about 24 oblong meatballs.

2. In the slow cooker insert, combine the olive oil and onion and spread to cover the bottom of the cooker. Top with the meatballs.

3. Pour in the chicken broth. Cover and cook for 7 hours on low.

→

FOR THE SAUCE

1 cup plain full-fat Greek yogurt

2 tablespoons tahini

1 tablespoon freshly squeezed lemon juice

½ teaspoon kosher salt

1 tablespoon extra-virgin olive oil

1 teaspoon za'atar (optional)

½ teaspoon ground sumac (optional)

TO MAKE THE SAUCE

1. In a small bowl, whisk together the yogurt, tahini, lemon juice, and salt.

2. Garnish the sauce with a drizzle of olive oil and a sprinkling of za'atar and sumac (if using). Serve the meatballs hot, with the sauce alongside for dipping.

Make It Paleo Omit the feta cheese and use a nondairy yogurt (such as coconut yogurt) in place of the regular yogurt.

Duck Legs Braised in Olive Oil with Chive Cream

Serves 4 to 6 • Prep: 10 minutes, plus overnight to brine • Cook: 6 hours on low

Duck slow cooked in fat (called duck confit) renders rich, succulent meat that is delicious as the centerpiece of a meal, topping an entrée salad, or as a filling for wraps, enchiladas, or other dishes. This type of dish is usually made with duck fat, which is expensive and can be hard to source. I like to use olive oil or coconut oil instead. Make some zucchini noodles to serve alongside this rich, meaty dish, if you like.

FOR THE SAUCE

1½ cups sour cream

3 tablespoons heavy (whipping) cream

¼ cup chopped fresh chives, plus additional for garnish

¾ teaspoon kosher salt

¼ teaspoon freshly ground black pepper

TO MAKE THE SAUCE

In a small bowl, stir together all the ingredients until well combined. Refrigerate until ready to use.

→

Macronutrients
Fat 75%
Protein 22%
Carbs 3%

Per Serving
Calories: 710
Total fat: 59g
Protein: 39g
Total carbs: 9g
Fiber: 2g
Net carbs: 7g
Sodium: 1,238mg
Cholesterol: 198mg

FOR THE DUCK

2 tablespoons kosher salt

4 garlic cloves, minced

4 duck legs

1 teaspoon freshly ground black pepper

4 to 5 cups extra-virgin olive oil or melted coconut oil

TO MAKE THE DUCK

1. Mash together the salt and garlic to make a paste. Rub the paste all over the duck legs. Arrange the duck in a single layer in a baking dish and season with the pepper. Cover the pan loosely with aluminum foil and refrigerate overnight.

2. Rinse the duck legs and pat them very dry with paper towels. Arrange the duck, skin-side up, in the slow cooker.

3. Pour the olive oil over the duck to cover it completely. Cover and cook for 6 hours on low.

4. When finished, remove the duck from the oil. Remove and discard the skin, pull the meat from the bones, and shred the meat.

5. Serve the meat topped with the cream sauce and garnish with additional chives.

Variation Tip It's a little extra work, but you don't have to toss all that oil after cooking. Instead, strain the oil after cooking the meat and then use it to make salad dressings or for cooking other savory dishes.

Slow-Cooked Duck
with Turnips in Cream

Serves 8 • Prep: 15 minutes • Cook: 7 hours on low

QUICK PREP

A whole duck makes a nice change from roasted chicken every once in a while. It's just as easy to cook in the slow cooker, but somehow seems a whole lot fancier. Turnips are a great low-carb alternative to potatoes and add a nice earthiness to this dish.

2 turnips, peeled and diced

2 celery stalks, diced

2 tablespoons unsalted butter or Ghee (page 179), melted

1 (3- to 4-pound) duck, giblets removed, rinsed and patted dry

1 teaspoon kosher salt

Freshly ground black pepper

2 tablespoons coconut oil

1 lemon, quartered

1 small onion, quartered

2 fresh rosemary sprigs

4 or 5 fresh thyme sprigs

¾ cup heavy (whipping) cream

Macronutrients
Fat 90%
Protein 9%
Carbs 1%

Per Serving
Calories: 831
Total fat: 83g
Protein: 20g
Total carbs: 3g
Fiber: 0g
Net carbs: 3g
Sodium: 413mg
Cholesterol: 172mg

1. In the slow cooker, toss the turnips and celery with the butter.

2. Generously season the duck with salt and pepper.

3. In a large skillet, heat the coconut oil over medium-high heat.

4. Add the duck, breast-side down, and cook until browned, about 5 minutes per side. Pierce the skin in several places with a small sharp knife or the tines of a fork.

5. Insert the lemon quarters, onion quarters, rosemary, and thyme into the duck cavity and place the duck, breast-side up, in the slow cooker on top of the vegetables. Cover and cook for 7 hours on low.

6. Remove the duck from the slow cooker and let it rest for about 10 minutes before carving.

7. While the duck is resting, stir the heavy cream into the juices and vegetables in the slow cooker. Serve the duck over the vegetables and sauce.

Variation Tip For a crispy skin, remove the cooked duck from the slow cooker and place it on a rack set in a roasting pan. Roast in a 425°F oven until browned and crisp, about 15 minutes.

Macronutrients
Fat 75%
Protein 19%
Carbs 6%

Per Serving
Calories: 910
Total fat: 78g
Protein: 39g
Total carbs: 13g
Fiber: 6g
Net carbs: 7g
Sodium: 1,093mg
Cholesterol: 48mg

Slow Cooker Carnitas Tacos

Serves 6 • Prep: 10 minutes • Cook: 7 hours on low

Traditional carnitas, the Mexican version of pulled pork, is deep-fried in a vat of lard. Cooking it in a slow cooker yields equally delicious results with much less mess. The meat is succulent and crispy around the edges, perfect for filling lettuce leaf tacos or low-carb burrito wraps, or for topping a salad.

1 onion, thinly sliced

4 garlic cloves, minced

¼ cup coconut oil, melted

1 tablespoon ground cumin

1 tablespoon fresh oregano

1 tablespoon chili powder

2 teaspoons kosher salt

1½ teaspoons freshly ground black pepper

2½ pounds boneless pork shoulder, top fatty layer scored in a crisscross pattern

½ cup water

1½ cups sour cream

12 large, crisp lettuce leaves

1 cup crumbled queso fresco or feta cheese

2 avocados, peeled, pitted, and sliced

Hot sauce or salsa (optional)

1. In the slow cooker, toss the onion slices and garlic with the coconut oil. Spread the vegetables in an even layer covering the bottom of the cooker.

2. In a small bowl, stir together the cumin, oregano, chili powder, salt, and pepper. Rub the spice mixture all over the pork and then place it in the slow cooker on top of the onions and garlic.

3. Add the water. Cover and cook for 7 hours on low.

4. Using two forks, shred the meat in the cooker and then stir it into the juices and onions to mix.

5. Stir in the sour cream.

6. Serve the meat spooned into the lettuce leaves, garnished with queso fresco, avocado, and hot sauce or salsa (if using).

Variation Tip Double this recipe and freeze the leftover pork in meal-size packets, so you'll always have a perfect low-carb protein on hand any time you want tacos, burritos, enchiladas, or other dishes.

Southeast Asian Lemongrass Pork

Serves 6 • Prep: 10 minutes, plus overnight to marinate • Cook: 8 hours on low

ALLERGEN-FREE

PALEO FRIENDLY

WORTH THE
EFFORT

Marinating pork in a flavorful seasoning mixture both tenderizes it and infuses it with flavor. It means you have to plan ahead a bit, but it's worth it. Wrap the meat in lettuce leaves with sliced fresh chiles and Southeast Asian herbs, such as mint, basil, and cilantro, or serve over cauliflower rice.

¼ cup coconut oil, melted

1 tablespoon apple cider vinegar

3 tablespoons minced lemongrass (white part only)

3 garlic cloves, minced

2 teaspoons kosher salt

1 teaspoon freshly ground black pepper

2 pounds boneless pork shoulder or butt roast, top fatty layer scored in a crisscross pattern

1 onion, sliced

1 (2-inch) piece fresh ginger, peeled and cut into thin slices

1 (14-ounce) can coconut milk

Macronutrients
Fat 71%
Protein 25%
Carbs 4%

Per Serving
Calories: 547
Total fat: 43g
Protein: 34g
Total carbs: 6g
Fiber: 2g
Net carbs: 4g
Sodium: 907mg
Cholesterol: 134mg

1. In a small bowl, stir together the coconut oil, cider vinegar, lemongrass, garlic, salt, and pepper.

2. Place the pork in a baking dish and rub the seasoning mixture all over it. Cover and refrigerate overnight.

3. In the morning, remove the pork from the refrigerator 30 to 60 minutes before you plan to cook it so it can come to room temperature. You could also complete the next step and then set a delay timer to start the slow cooker 30 to 60 minutes later, if you prefer.

4. Cover the bottom of the slow cooker with the onion and ginger slices in an even layer. Top with the marinated pork, along with any accumulated juices in the dish.

5. Pour the coconut milk over the top. Cover and cook for 8 hours on low.

6. Shred the meat using two forks. Serve immediately, refrigerate for up to 3 days, or freeze for up to 3 months.

Variation Tip You can place the onions and garlic in the slow cooker, rub the pork with the seasoning mixture and place it in the slow cooker, and then cover and refrigerate the whole thing overnight. Just be sure to let the ceramic insert come to room temperature before turning on the slow cooker.

Macronutrients
Fat 64%
Protein 33%
Carbs 3%

Per Serving
Calories: 524
Total fat: 36g
Protein: 44g
Total carbs: 6g
Fiber: 1g
Net carbs: 5g
Sodium: 1,250mg
Cholesterol: 129mg

Slow-Cooked Pork Loin with Creamy Gravy

Serves 6 • Prep: 10 minutes • Cook: 8 hours on low

A pork loin roast makes for a classic and comforting Sunday dinner. This one is so easy to make, you can have it any night of the week. Just a handful of ingredients give it flavor, and a long, slow cook (while you're off doing your own thing) renders it tender and juicy, and with a ready-made gravy to boot.

1 tablespoon kosher salt

2 teaspoons freshly ground black pepper

4 garlic cloves, minced

1 (3-pound) bone-in pork loin roast

2 onions, sliced

¼ cup water

2 tablespoons soy sauce or tamari

1 cup heavy (whipping) cream

1. In a small bowl, stir together the salt, pepper, and garlic to form a paste. Rub the seasoning mixture all over the pork roast.

2. Arrange the onions in the bottom of the slow cooker. Pour in the water and soy sauce. Place the roast on top of the onions. Cover and cook for 8 hours on low.

3. Remove the roast from the slow cooker and let it rest for 10 minutes.

4. While the roast is resting, transfer the remaining liquid and onions from the slow cooker to a blender. Add the heavy cream and process into a smooth sauce.

5. Slice the pork and serve it with the gravy spooned over the top.

Make It Paleo Substitute unsweetened almond milk for the cream and coconut aminos for the soy sauce.

Mustard-Herb Pork Chops

Serves 4 • Prep: 5 minutes • Cook: 8 hours on low or 4 hours on high

With very little prep, this is a great fix-it-and-forget-it dish. Pop everything in the slow cooker before work and come home to juicy, delicious pork chops. A quick spin in the blender and some added cream turns the cooking juices into a rich sauce. This recipe is easily doubled if you have more people to feed or want leftovers.

¾ cup chicken or beef broth

2 tablespoons coconut oil, melted

1 tablespoon Dijon mustard

2 garlic cloves, minced

1 tablespoon paprika

1 tablespoon onion powder

1 teaspoon dried oregano

1 teaspoon dried basil

1 teaspoon dried parsley

1 onion, thinly sliced

4 thick-cut boneless pork chops

1 cup heavy (whipping) cream

Macronutrients
Fat 62%
Protein 33%
Carbs 5%

Per Serving
Calories: 470
Total fat: 32g
Protein: 39g
Total carbs: 7g
Fiber: 2g
Net carbs: 5g
Sodium: 425mg
Cholesterol: 132mg

1. In the slow cooker, stir together the broth, coconut oil, mustard, garlic, paprika, onion powder, oregano, basil, and parsley.

2. Add the onion and pork chops and toss to coat. Cover and cook for 8 hours on low or 4 hours on high.

3. Transfer the chops to a serving platter. Transfer the remaining juices and onion in the slow cooker to a blender, add the heavy cream, and process until smooth. Pour the sauce over the pork chops and serve hot.

Make It Allergen-Free/Paleo Substitute a dairy-free sour cream or full-fat coconut milk for the cream.

Macronutrients
Fat 67%
Protein 22%
Carbs 11%

Per Serving
Calories: 488
Total fat: 40g
Protein: 27g
Total carbs: 5g
Fiber: 1g
Net carbs: 4g
Sodium: 911mg
Cholesterol: 145mg

Pork Loin with Ginger Cream Sauce

Serves 6 • Prep: 15 minutes • Cook: 8 hours on low

This spicy, rich pork roast recipe is great for any night of the week. The ginger and cinnamon give it a kick of warm spice and the rich cream ties it all together. Serve it with cauliflower rice or zucchini noodles.

FOR THE PORK

1 tablespoon erythritol

2 teaspoons kosher salt

1 teaspoon garlic powder

1 teaspoon ground ginger

½ teaspoon ground cinnamon

½ teaspoon ground cloves

½ teaspoon red pepper flakes

¼ teaspoon freshly ground black pepper

1 (2-pound) pork shoulder roast

½ cup water

TO MAKE THE PORK

1. In a small bowl, stir together the erythritol, salt, garlic powder, ginger, cinnamon, cloves, red pepper flakes, and black pepper. Rub the seasoning mixture all over the pork and place it in the slow cooker.

2. Pour the water into the cooker around the pork. Cover and cook for 8 hours on low.

3. Remove the pork from the slow cooker and let it rest for about 5 minutes.

FOR THE SAUCE

2 tablespoons unsalted butter

3 tablespoons minced fresh ginger

2 shallots, minced

1 tablespoon minced garlic

⅔ cup dry white wine

1 cup heavy (whipping) cream

TO MAKE THE SAUCE

1. While the pork rests, melt the butter in a small saucepan over medium heat.

2. Stir in the ginger, shallots, and garlic.

3. Add the white wine and bring to a boil. Cook, stirring, until the liquid is reduced to about ¼ cup, about 5 minutes.

4. Whisk in the heavy cream and continue to boil, stirring, until the sauce thickens, 3 to 5 minutes more.

5. Slice the pork and serve it with the sauce spooned over the top.

Make It Allergen-Free/Paleo Substitute coconut oil for the butter and full-fat coconut milk for the heavy cream. For paleo, substitute coconut sugar for the erythritol and chicken broth for the wine.

Macronutrients

Fat 70%

Protein 19%

Carbs 11%

Per Serving

Calories: 486

Total fat: 38g

Protein: 22g

Total carbs: 14g

Fiber: 4g

Net carbs: 10g

Sodium: 2,211mg

Cholesterol: 126mg

Smoked Sausage
with Cabbage & Onions

Serves 6 · Prep: 5 minutes · Cook: 7 hours on low

This is the kind of comfort food my grandmother used to make, and I wouldn't be surprised if yours made something similar. With just 5 minutes of prep and a full day in the slow cooker, this becomes a complete—and delicious—meal. Add a bit of butter to the hot cabbage for extra flavor.

1 tablespoon extra-virgin olive oil

1½ pounds cabbage, cut into wedges

1 onion, halved and thinly sliced

½ teaspoon kosher salt

½ teaspoon freshly ground black pepper

1 cup chicken broth

¼ cup (½ stick) unsalted butter or Ghee (page 179), melted

1 tablespoon spicy brown mustard

2 pounds smoked pork sausage, such as kielbasa, cut into 3-inch lengths

1. Coat the inside of the slow cooker insert with the olive oil.

2. Put the cabbage wedges and onions in the slow cooker. Sprinkle with salt and pepper and then add the chicken broth, butter, and mustard. Toss to coat the cabbage and onions.

3. Top with the sausage pieces. Cover and cook for 7 hours on low. Serve hot.

Variation Tip Use any type of sausage you like for this, including beef or chicken sausage. You might try using hot links, andouille, or linguiça, if you like those.

Spice-Rubbed Pork Belly
with Brussels Sprouts & Turnips

Serves 6 to 8 • Prep: 10 minutes • Cook: 8 hours on low

This flavorful pork belly dish is a full meal on its own, but it also makes a great filling for wraps or lettuce leaves, or toss it into scrambled eggs for a dinner-for-breakfast—or breakfast-for-dinner—option.

2 tablespoons paprika

2 tablespoons onion powder

2 tablespoons garlic powder

1 tablespoon kosher salt

1 tablespoon freshly ground black pepper

2 pounds pork belly, thickly sliced

1 pound Brussels sprouts, halved

1 medium turnip, peeled and diced

4 bay leaves

Macronutrients
Fat 85%
Protein 9%
Carbs 6%

Per Serving
Calories: 848
Total fat: 80g
Protein: 18g
Total carbs: 14g
Fiber: 5g
Net carbs: 9g
Sodium: 1,223mg
Cholesterol: 109mg

1. In a small bowl, stir together the paprika, onion powder, garlic powder, salt, and pepper. Rub the mixture all over the pork belly slices.

2. In the bottom of the slow cooker, arrange the Brussels sprouts, turnip, and bay leaves in an even layer.

3. Lay the pork over the vegetables. Cover and cook for 8 hours on low.

4. Discard the bay leaves and serve hot.

Variation Tip Marinating the pork overnight in the spice rub means you have to plan ahead, but it makes for really flavorful meat. After completing step 1, wrap the pork belly tightly in plastic wrap, along with the bay leaves, and refrigerate overnight.

Macronutrients
Fat 68%
Protein 25%
Carbs 7%

Per Serving
Calories: 951
Total fat: 70g
Protein: 63g
Total carbs: 22g
Fiber: 7g
Net carbs: 15g
Sodium: 1,892mg
Cholesterol: 250mg

Pork & Sausage Meatballs with Mushroom Ragout

Serves 4 • Prep: 20 minutes • Cook: 8 hours on low

Combining pork and pork sausage to make meatballs is genius. They are meaty and spiked with the savory flavors of garlic, fennel, Parmesan cheese, and more. Dried porcini mushrooms add intense umami flavor to the sauce. If you can't find them, substitute 1 cup sliced or diced fresh cremini mushrooms. Serve this dish over spaghetti squash or zucchini noodles.

FOR THE MEATBALLS

1½ pounds sweet Italian sausage, casings removed

8 ounces ground pork

1 cup almond meal

½ cup pine nuts

2 cups finely grated Parmesan cheese, divided

1 large egg, beaten

1 teaspoon rubbed sage

1 teaspoon dried oregano

½ teaspoon kosher salt

¼ teaspoon freshly grated nutmeg

TO MAKE THE MEATBALLS

1. In a large bowl, thoroughly mix the sausage, ground pork, almond meal, and pine nuts.

2. Add 1 cup of Parmesan cheese, egg, sage, oregano, salt, and nutmeg. Mix well. Form the mixture into 12 meatballs.

FOR THE SAUCE

¼ cup (½ stick) unsalted butter, melted

1 (14.5-ounce) can diced tomatoes, with juice

¼ cup tomato paste

½ ounce dried porcini mushrooms, crumbled

1 teaspoon dried oregano

1 teaspoon dried thyme

½ teaspoon fennel seeds

½ teaspoon kosher salt

¼ teaspoon red pepper flakes

1 cup heavy (whipping) cream

TO MAKE THE SAUCE

1. In the slow cooker, stir together the butter, tomatoes and their juice, tomato paste, mushrooms, oregano, thyme, fennel seeds, salt, and red pepper flakes. Nestle the meatballs in the sauce. Cover and cook for 8 hours on low.

2. Just before serving, stir in the heavy cream. Serve hot, garnished with the remaining 1 cup of Parmesan cheese.

Make It Paleo Substitute additional almond meal for the Parmesan cheese in the meatballs. In the sauce, substitute coconut oil for the butter and full-fat coconut milk or dairy-free sour cream for the heavy cream. Garnish with toasted and ground almonds and nutritional yeast instead of the Parmesan cheese.

SIX

Beef & Lamb Dishes

Macronutrients
Fat 75%
Protein 17%
Carbs 8%

Per Serving
Calories: 787
Total fat: 68g
Protein: 28g
Total carbs: 17g
Fiber: 2g
Net carbs: 15g
Sodium: 1,209mg
Cholesterol: 175mg

Spaghetti Squash Bolognese

Serves 6 • Prep: 15 minutes • Cook: 6 hours on low

Few things are more welcome at the end of a long day than a steaming bowl of spaghetti with rich, tomatoey meat sauce. This low-carb version starts with flavorful pancetta and ground beef, is enriched with cream, and then gets served over spaghetti squash noodles.

1 pound (70% lean) ground beef

6 ounces pancetta or bacon, diced

1 small onion, diced

2 garlic cloves, minced

2 tablespoons unsalted butter or Ghee (page 179)

1 (14.5-ounce) can diced tomatoes, with juice

½ cup chicken or beef broth

2 tablespoons tomato paste

1 teaspoon dried oregano

1 teaspoon dried basil

1 teaspoon kosher salt

½ teaspoon freshly ground black pepper

½ teaspoon red pepper flakes (optional)

1 spaghetti squash, halved, seeds and pulp removed

½ cup heavy (whipping) cream

1 cup grated Parmesan cheese

1. In a large skillet, cook the ground beef and pancetta over medium-high heat until browned, about 5 minutes. Using a slotted spoon, transfer the meat to the slow cooker, leaving behind the rendered fat.

2. Return the skillet to medium-high heat. Add the onion and sauté until softened, about 5 minutes.

3. Stir in the garlic and sauté for 30 seconds more.

4. Add the butter and stir until melted. Transfer the onion and garlic mixture to the slow cooker.

5. Add the tomatoes and their juice, broth, tomato paste, oregano, basil, salt, pepper, and red pepper flakes (if using) and stir to combine.

6. Place the squash in the slow cooker, cut-side down. Cover and cook for 6 hours on low.

7. Carefully remove the squash from the cooker and use a fork to shred the strands.

8. Stir the heavy cream into the sauce.

9. Serve the spaghetti squash like noodles, topped with the sauce and garnished with the Parmesan cheese.

Variation Tip If you have trouble fitting the squash in the slow cooker with the sauce, don't panic! When the sauce is ready, halve and seed the squash and then place it in a microwave-safe baking dish, cut-side down. Add 1 inch of water to the dish and micro-wave for 10 to 12 minutes on high.

Macronutrients
Fat 70%
Protein 21%
Carbs 9%

Per Serving
Calories: 598
Total fat: 46g
Protein: 32g
Total carbs: 14g
Fiber: 4g
Net carbs: 10g
Sodium: 1,738mg
Cholesterol: 107mg

Meatballs in
Smoky Chipotle Sauce

Serves 6 • Prep: 15 minutes • Cook: 6 hours on low

These Mexican-style meatballs, or *albondigas*, are flavored with smoky chipotle powder and Mexican queso fresco (feta cheese makes a fine substitute if you can't find queso fresco). The spicy tomato-based sauce is thickened with sour cream. Serve this dish steaming hot in soup bowls, garnished with diced avocado and more cheese.

FOR THE SAUCE

1 cup chicken broth or water

1 (14.5-ounce) can diced tomatoes, with juice

1 (4-ounce) can fire-roasted diced green chiles, with juice

¼ cup (½ stick) unsalted butter, cubed

2 tablespoons tomato paste

½ onion, diced

2 garlic cloves, minced

1 teaspoon ground cumin

1 teaspoon ground coriander

1 teaspoon dried oregano

1 teaspoon ground chipotle

¾ teaspoon kosher salt

1 cup sour cream

⅓ cup crumbled queso fresco, for garnish

1 avocado, peeled, pitted, and diced, for garnish

TO MAKE THE SAUCE

In the slow cooker, combine the chicken broth, tomatoes and their juice, green chiles and their juice, butter, tomato paste, onion, garlic, cumin, coriander, oregano, chipotle, and salt. Stir to mix well.

FOR THE MEATBALLS

1½ pounds (70% lean) ground beef

¾ cup crumbled queso fresco

1 large egg, beaten

½ onion, diced

2 garlic cloves, minced

2 teaspoons kosher salt

1 teaspoon ground cumin

1 teaspoon ground coriander

½ teaspoon freshly ground black pepper

¼ teaspoon ground allspice

TO MAKE THE MEATBALLS

1. In a large bowl, mix all the ingredients. Form the meat into about 30 (2-inch) balls, adding them to the sauce in the cooker as they are formed. Cover and cook for 6 hours on low.

2. Just before serving, stir the sour cream into the sauce.

3. Serve hot, topped with crumbled queso fresco and diced avocado.

Variation Tip If you have extra time, brown the meatballs in a skillet in hot coconut oil before adding them to the sauce in the slow cooker. This step isn't necessary, but it adds depth of flavor and helps the meatballs hold together better in the sauce.

Macronutrients
Fat 73%
Protein 22%
Carbs 5%

Per Serving
Calories: 667
Total fat: 55g
Protein: 35g
Total carbs: 9g
Fiber: 3g
Net carbs: 6g
Sodium: 1,483mg
Cholesterol: 186mg

Meatballs in Tomato Sauce with Mozzarella & Basil

Serves 8 • Prep: 20 minutes • Cook: 7 hours on low

Ground beef and Italian sausage make a great base for savory meatballs. Riced cauliflower and ground almonds stand in for the usual bread crumbs or rice. (To prepare the riced cauliflower, trim off the root, chop the cauliflower into chunks, and pulse in a food processor until it is the texture of rice.) These meaty morsels are cooked in rich tomato sauce and finished with melty fresh mozzarella cheese and fresh basil. Serve this over zucchini or crookneck squash noodles or spaghetti squash.

FOR THE SAUCE

¼ cup (½ stick) unsalted butter, melted

1 (28-ounce) can diced tomatoes, with juice

1 tablespoon extra-virgin olive oil

2 garlic cloves, minced

2 teaspoons dried basil

1 teaspoon dried parsley

1 teaspoon kosher salt

½ teaspoon freshly ground black pepper

TO MAKE THE SAUCE

In the slow cooker, stir together all the ingredients.

Make It Paleo Use coconut oil or olive oil in place of the butter in the sauce. Omit the Parmesan cheese and double the quantity of almond meal in the meatballs. Omit the mozzarella cheese and top with cashew cream instead.

FOR THE MEATBALLS

2 large eggs

2 cups riced cauliflower

2 cups grated Parmesan cheese, divided

½ cup almond meal

1½ tablespoons Italian seasoning

1 teaspoon kosher salt

½ teaspoon freshly ground black pepper

½ teaspoon garlic powder

1 pound (70% lean) ground beef

12 ounces Italian sausage, casings removed

8 ounces fresh mozzarella cheese, thinly sliced

¼ cup sliced fresh basil leaves

TO MAKE THE MEATBALLS

1. In a large bowl, beat the eggs, then whisk in the cauliflower, 1 cup of Parmesan cheese, almond meal, Italian seasoning, salt, pepper, and garlic powder.

2. Add the ground beef and sausage and mix to combine. Form the mixture into 24 (1-inch) balls, placing them in the slow cooker as they are formed. Cover and cook for 7 hours on low.

3. About 15 minutes before serving, scatter the mozzarella cheese over the top of the meatballs and sauce. Cover and continue to cook until the cheese melts, about 15 minutes more. Serve hot, garnished with the remaining 1 cup of Parmesan cheese and the basil leaves.

Macronutrients
Fat 70%
Protein 25%
Carbs 5%

Per Serving
Calories: 508
Total fat: 40g
Protein: 32g
Total carbs: 5g
Fiber: 1g
Net carbs: 4g
Sodium: 908mg
Cholesterol: 106mg

Italian Stuffed Meatloaf

Serves 8 • Prep: 10 minutes • Cook: 6 hours on low or 3 hours on high

Meatloaf is one of my favorite comfort foods, both as a cook and as an eater. It's easy to make, versatile in terms of how you flavor it, and deeply satisfying. This one surprises with a hidden center of melty cheese and olives. Serve it with buttery mashed cauliflower for an old-school meal that's low in carbs. Leftovers make a great filling for lettuce wraps—just add a bit of mayonnaise and sliced tomato.

1 pound (70% lean) ground beef

1 pound Italian sausage, casings removed

1 large egg, lightly beaten

1 cup sour cream

½ cup almond meal

½ onion, finely diced

4 garlic cloves, minced

2 tablespoons tomato paste

2 teaspoons dried oregano

1 teaspoon kosher salt

1 teaspoon freshly ground black pepper

1½ cups shredded fontina cheese

½ cup grated Parmesan cheese, divided

½ cup pitted, sliced olives

Extra-virgin olive oil, for coating the aluminum foil

1. In a large bowl, mix the beef, sausage, egg, sour cream, almond meal, onion, garlic, tomato paste, oregano, salt, and pepper.

2. In a separate bowl, toss together the fontina cheese, ¼ cup of Parmesan cheese, and the olives.

3. Lay out a piece of foil large enough to line the cooker and create a sling to help you remove the cooked meatloaf. Coat it with olive oil.

4. Form half of the meat mixture into a flat loaf in the center of the foil. Scatter the cheese and olive mixture in a strip down the center of the loaf. Top with the remaining meat mixture, enclosing the cheese and olives in the center of the meatloaf.

5. Sprinkle the remaining ¼ cup of Parmesan over the top.

6. Using the foil sling, lift the loaf and lower it into the slow cooker. Cover and cook for 6 hours on low or 3 hours on high.

7. Use the foil sling to carefully remove the loaf from the slow cooker and transfer it to a serving platter. Let the loaf rest for at least 5 minutes before slicing. Serve hot.

Variation Tip If you have a little extra time before serving, leave the Parmesan off the top of the loaf and, once the cooking is finished, turn off the slow cooker and spread ½ cup of thick tomato sauce or low-carb ketchup over the top of the meatloaf and sprinkle ½ cup of shredded cheese (I use a mixture of fontina and Parmesan) over the top. Place the lid back on the slow cooker and let the meatloaf sit until the cheese melts, about 10 minutes.

Macronutrients
Fat 75%
Protein 19%
Carbs 6%

Per Serving
Calories: 681
Total fat: 57g
Protein: 29g
Total carbs: 13g
Fiber: 4g
Net carbs: 9g
Sodium: 2,070mg
Cholesterol: 165mg

Classic Corned Beef & Cabbage with Horseradish Cream

Serves 8 to 10 • Prep: 10 minutes • Cook: 8 hours on low

Corned beef is a great cut of meat to cook in the slow cooker. Like other inexpensive cuts, brisket needs to be cooked for a long time to become tender. That's exactly the kind of thing the slow cooker was invented for. A simple spice mixture, a few chopped veggies, and a corned beef brisket is all you need. This recipe makes a lot, so plan to serve it to crowd, or get ready to enjoy leftovers all week.

FOR THE HORSERADISH CREAM
1½ cups sour cream
1 cup prepared horseradish
2 tablespoons Dijon mustard

1½ teaspoons white wine vinegar
1 teaspoon kosher salt
½ teaspoon freshly ground black pepper

TO MAKE THE HORSERADISH CREAM

In a medium bowl, stir together all the ingredients. Cover and chill until ready to serve.

Variation Tip For the best flavor, substitute fresh horseradish root if you can find it. Peel the root and grate it using the small holes of a box grater or a Microplane grater. Replace the 1 cup prepared horseradish with ½ cup freshly grated.

FOR THE BEEF

1 head cabbage, cut into wedges

1 onion, chopped

½ cup (1 stick) unsalted butter or Ghee (page 179), melted

1½ cups water

½ teaspoon ground coriander

½ teaspoon ground mustard

½ teaspoon ground allspice

½ teaspoon ground marjoram

½ teaspoon ground thyme

½ teaspoon kosher salt

½ teaspoon freshly ground black pepper

1 (3-pound) corned beef brisket

TO MAKE THE BEEF

1. In the slow cooker, toss together the cabbage wedges, onion, and butter, and then spread them out in an even layer. Add the water.

2. In a small bowl, stir together the coriander, mustard, allspice, marjoram, thyme, salt, and pepper. Rub the spice mixture all over the corned beef. Place the beef on top of the vegetables in the slow cooker. Cover and cook for 8 hours on low.

3. Let the meat rest for 5 to 10 minutes before slicing. Serve with the vegetables and horseradish cream.

Per Serving
Calories: 895
Total fat: 73g
Protein: 38g
Total carbs: 16g
Fiber: 3g
Net carbs: 13g
Sodium: 2,830mg
Cholesterol: 168mg

Braised Beef Short Ribs with Juniper Berries & Mascarpone Sauce

Serves 4 • Prep: 10 minutes • Cook: 8 hours on low

With a long, slow braise, short ribs become meltingly, fall-off-the-bone tender. Flavored with pancetta and juniper berries, cooked over a bed of onions and fennel, and bathed in a rich, creamy mascarpone sauce, this will likely become your go-to special occasion meal. Serve over goat cheese–enriched mashed cauliflower.

4 ounces pancetta, diced

½ cup diced tomatoes

1 fennel bulb, diced

1 onion, chopped

4 garlic cloves, minced

2 meaty beef short ribs

1 tablespoon kosher salt

2 teaspoons freshly ground black pepper

10 juniper berries, smashed with the side of a knife

2 bay leaves

1½ cups beef broth

½ cup dry red wine

¼ cup tomato paste

2 cups mascarpone cheese

1 cup grated Parmesan cheese

1. In the slow cooker, toss together the pancetta, tomatoes, fennel, onion, and garlic. Spread these in an even layer over the bottom of the slow cooker.

2. Generously season the beef ribs all over with the salt and pepper. Nestle them on top of the vegetables in the cooker. Scatter the juniper berries and bay leaves over the top.

3. In a medium bowl, whisk together the beef broth, red wine, and tomato paste. Pour this over the meat. Cover and cook for 8 hours on low.

4. Transfer the ribs to a plate. Pull the meat from the bones with two forks, shred it, and return the meat to the cooker.

5. Stir the mascarpone and Parmesan cheeses into the sauce. Discard the bay leaves and serve hot.

Variation Tip If you don't mind spending a little extra time on prep, cook the pancetta in a skillet over medium-high heat until nicely browned. Add the fennel, onion, and garlic and cook until they begin to soften. Transfer the mixture to the slow cooker, then proceed with the recipe as written.

Carne Asada Tacos

Serves 4 • Prep: 10 minutes • Cook: 8 hours on low

Flank steak is a very flavorful cut, perfect for making meaty tacos. Here, it is coated with Mexican spices and slow cooked to perfection. Served in crunchy lettuce leaves topped with all the usual taco fixins, it makes for a filling, low-carb Mexican meal.

1 onion, diced

1 red bell pepper, seeded and diced

4 garlic cloves, minced

1 (1½-pound) flank steak

1 teaspoon ground cumin

1 teaspoon chili powder

1 teaspoon smoked paprika

1 teaspoon kosher salt

Juice of 1 orange

Juice of 2 limes

⅓ cup beef broth

12 large, crisp lettuce leaves

1½ cups sour cream

1 cup crumbled queso fresco or feta cheese

2 avocados, peeled, pitted, and diced

Hot sauce or salsa, for serving (optional)

1. In the slow cooker, toss together the onion, red bell pepper, and garlic.

2. Season the steak all over with the cumin, chili powder, paprika, and salt. Lay the steak on top of the vegetables in the cooker.

3. Sprinkle with the orange juice and lime juice and add the beef broth. Cover and cook for 8 hours on low.

4. Use two forks to shred the meat and then toss it with the vegetables in the slow cooker.

5. Serve stuffed into lettuce leaves and topped with sour cream, queso fresco, avocado, and hot sauce or salsa (if using).

Variation Tip Use the cooked meat for these low-carb nachos: Seed and slice 3 or 4 bell peppers (various colors) into wedges. Toss them with a bit of olive oil and roast them in a 400°F oven until they begin to brown, about 20 minutes. Spoon the cooked and shredded steak mixture onto the wedges, top with shredded cheese, and broil until the cheese melts. Serve with sour cream and diced avocado or guacamole, if desired.

Macronutrients
Fat 69%
Protein 22%
Carbs 9%

Per Serving
Calories: 761
Total fat: 57g
Protein: 42g
Total carbs: 20g
Fiber: 8g
Net carbs: 12g
Sodium: 1,120mg
Cholesterol: 134mg

BEEF & LAMB DISHES

Macronutrients
Fat 70%
Protein 23%
Carbs 7%

Per Serving
Calories: 782
Total fat: 60g
Protein: 45g
Total carbs: 20g
Fiber: 6g
Net carbs: 14g
Sodium: 1,770mg
Cholesterol: 201mg

Beef-Stuffed Cabbage in Creamy Tomato Sauce

Serves 4 • Prep: 20 minutes • Cook: 8 hours on low or 4 hours on high

Stuffed cabbage is a favorite dish of Jewish grandmothers (my own included), and always a crowd pleaser. Most versions include rice in the filling, but this version substitutes almond meal, and adds bacon for extra fatty goodness (with apologies to my Jewish grandmother). I've substituted erythritol or stevia for the sugar that's usually used for the sweet-and-sour sauce, but you can leave it out if you prefer a tarter, more savory sauce.

1 pound (70% lean) ground beef

4 bacon slices, finely diced

1 cup shredded Gruyère cheese

1 small onion, finely diced

1 large egg, beaten

½ cup almond meal

1 teaspoon garlic powder

1 teaspoon kosher salt

¼ teaspoon freshly ground black pepper

12 whole cabbage leaves, lightly steamed in the microwave

1 (14.5-ounce) can tomato sauce

1 tablespoon red wine vinegar or apple cider vinegar

2 teaspoons soy sauce or tamari

1 teaspoon erythritol or ⅓ teaspoon stevia powder

1 teaspoon paprika

¼ teaspoon ground allspice

1½ cups sour cream

1. In a large bowl, mix the ground beef, bacon, Gruyère cheese, onion, egg, almond meal, garlic powder, salt, and pepper.

2. Place a handful of the meat mixture in the center of each of the softened cabbage leaves, dividing equally. Fold two sides of the leaf over the filling, and then roll it up like a burrito. Place each roll, seam-side down, in the slow cooker (it's okay to stack the rolls if necessary).

3. In a medium bowl, stir together the tomato sauce, vinegar, soy sauce, erythritol, paprika, and allspice. Pour the sauce mixture over the rolls. Cover and cook for 8 hours on low or 4 hours on high.

4. Turn off the slow cooker and let the cabbage rolls rest for 10 to 15 minutes.

5. Carefully remove the cabbage rolls from the slow cooker and arrange them on a serving platter. Stir the sour cream into the sauce in the cooker, then pour it over the cabbage rolls. Serve warm.

Variation Tip If filling the rolls seems like too much work, just make the meat mixture into small meatballs instead. Chop the cabbage and add it to the cooker along with the rest of the tomato sauce ingredients.

Per Serving
Calories: 625
Total fat: 48g
Protein: 38g
Total carbs: 12g
Fiber: 4g
Net carbs: 8g
Sodium: 2,650mg
Cholesterol: 65mg

Beef with Peanut Sauce

Serves 4 • Prep: 10 minutes • Cook: 8 hours on low

Skirt steak is a great cut of meat for cooking in the slow cooker. It's nicely marbled, which gives it deep flavor, and it becomes very tender as it cooks. The peanut dipping sauce is addictively sweet and spicy.

FOR THE STEAK

½ cup soy sauce or tamari

2 tablespoons water

2 tablespoons dry sherry or dry white wine

1 teaspoon blackstrap molasses

2 garlic cloves, minced

1 tablespoon minced fresh ginger

1½ teaspoons stevia powder

1 pound skirt steak, cubed

2 tablespoons toasted sesame oil

FOR THE SAUCE

¾ cup coconut cream

½ cup all-natural peanut butter

½ cup water

2 tablespoons soy sauce or tamari

1 tablespoon freshly squeezed lime juice

1 garlic clove, minced

1 tablespoon erythritol or pinch stevia powder

½ teaspoon chili paste or red pepper flakes

TO MAKE THE STEAK

1. In the slow cooker, stir together the soy sauce, water, sherry, molasses, garlic, ginger, and stevia powder.

2. Drizzle the steak with the sesame oil and add it to the slow cooker. Toss to coat the meat with the sauce. Cover and cook for 8 hours on low.

TO MAKE THE SAUCE

1. In a small saucepan set over medium heat, combine the coconut cream, peanut butter, water, soy sauce, lime juice, garlic, erythritol, and chili paste. Heat, stirring frequently, until the peanut butter melts and the sauce is a uniform consistency.

2. Serve the meat hot, with the peanut sauce for dipping.

Variation Tip If you'd like to add some green vegetables to this one-pot meal, cut a head of broccoli into florets and add it to the slow cooker 30 minutes before the end of the cooking time.

Cheesesteak Casserole with Peppers, Mushrooms & Onions

Serves 6 • Prep: 15 minutes • Cook: 8 hours on low

This is everything you love about a Philly cheesesteak—minus the high-carb hoagie roll. You can serve this dish in bowls as a cheese-topped stew or casserole, or use it to fill low-carb wraps to get closer to the real cheesesteak experience.

2 tablespoons coconut oil

1 onion, thinly sliced

8 ounces cremini or button mushrooms, sliced

1 green bell pepper, seeded and cut into strips

1 red bell pepper, seeded and cut into strips

1½ pounds rib eye steak

¾ teaspoon kosher salt

¾ teaspoon freshly ground black pepper

8 ounces provolone cheese, thinly sliced

Macronutrients
Fat 72%
Protein 24%
Carbs 4%

Per Serving
Calories: 734
Total fat: 59g
Protein: 43g
Total carbs: 8g
Fiber: 2g
Net carbs: 6g
Sodium: 1,005mg
Cholesterol: 135mg

1. In a large skillet, heat the coconut oil over medium-high heat. Add the onion and sauté until beginning to soften, about 3 minutes.

2. Add the mushrooms and continue to sauté until the mushrooms begin to brown, about 5 minutes. Transfer the mixture to the slow cooker.

3. Add the green and red bell peppers to the slow cooker and stir to mix.

4. Return the skillet to medium-high heat. Season the steak with the salt and pepper and add it to the skillet. Cook until browned, about 2 minutes per side. Transfer the steak to the slow cooker, placing it on top of the vegetables. Cover and cook for 8 hours on low.

5. Remove the steak from the cooker and let it rest for a couple of minutes. Leave the slow cooker on and keep it covered. After a few minutes, slice the steak into thin strips and return them to the slow cooker. Place the provolone cheese over the top, replace the cover, and let it sit for a few minutes until the cheese is melty. Serve hot.

Variation Tip After slicing the steak, transfer the vegetables from the slow cooker to a baking dish. Place the sliced steak on top, top with the cheese, and broil for 3 to 4 minutes until the cheese is melted and bubbly.

BEEF & LAMB DISHES

Macronutrients

Fat 71%

Protein 25%

Carbs 4%

Per Serving

Calories: 594

Total fat: 47g

Protein: 35g

Total carbs: 7g

Fiber: 1g

Net carbs: 6g

Sodium: 581mg

Cholesterol: 142mg

Creamy Beef Stroganoff with Mushrooms & Bacon

Serves 6 • Prep: 10 minutes • Cook: 8 hours on low

Quick to make, very low in carbs, and full of delicious flavor from the beef, mushrooms, bacon, and sour cream, this is one of my go-to slow cooker meals for busy weeks, especially during the colder months when I really want something hearty at the end of the day. You could serve it with steamed green beans or over zucchini noodles or spaghetti squash.

2 pounds beef stew meat, cut into 1-inch cubes

4 bacon slices, diced

8 ounces cremini or button mushrooms, quartered

1 onion, halved and sliced

2 garlic cloves, minced

1 cup beef broth

¼ cup tomato paste

1 teaspoon smoked paprika

½ teaspoon kosher salt

¼ teaspoon freshly ground black pepper

1½ cups sour cream

2 tablespoons minced fresh parsley

1. In the slow cooker, stir together the beef, bacon, mushrooms, onion, garlic, beef broth, tomato paste, paprika, salt, and pepper. Cover and cook for 8 hours on low.

2. Just before serving, stir in the sour cream. Serve hot, garnished with the parsley.

Make It Allergen-Free/Paleo Substitute full-fat plain cultured coconut yogurt for the sour cream.

Cajun Beef & Sausage
Stuffed Peppers

Serves 6 • Prep: 10 minutes • Cook: 7 hours on low

Macronutrients
Fat 70%
Protein 20%
Carbs 10%

Flavored with a classic Cajun spice mix of oregano, cayenne pepper, paprika, garlic, and onion, these meaty stuffed peppers have a spicy kick. The andouille sausage adds smokiness and even more Cajun flavor, but you can substitute any type of cooked sausage you like.

Per Serving
Calories: 325
Total fat: 25g
Protein: 16g
Total carbs: 9g
Fiber: 4g
Net carbs: 5g
Sodium: 639mg
Cholesterol: 37mg

12 ounces (70% lean) ground beef

12 ounces andouille sausage, finely diced

1½ cups shredded Cheddar cheese, divided

½ cup almond meal

2 celery stalks, finely diced

1 onion, finely diced

4 garlic cloves, minced

1 teaspoon dried oregano

1 teaspoon paprika

1 teaspoon kosher salt

½ teaspoon freshly ground black pepper

¼ teaspoon cayenne pepper

3 bell peppers (any color), halved through the stem, seeded and ribbed

¼ cup beef broth

1. In a large bowl, mix the beef, sausage, 1 cup of Cheddar cheese, almond meal, celery, onion, garlic, oregano, paprika, salt, black pepper, and cayenne pepper. Spoon the meat mixture into the pepper halves, dividing equally. Place the stuffed peppers in the slow cooker.

2. Pour the beef broth around the peppers.

3. Sprinkle with the remaining ½ cup of Cheddar cheese. Cover and cook for 7 hours on low. Serve hot.

Variation Tip You can give these peppers an Italian flavor by substituting sweet Italian sausage for the andouille, substituting an Italian cheese, such as Asiago or fontina, for the Cheddar, adding a few tablespoons of tomato paste to the meat mixture, and omitting the celery and paprika.

Macronutrients
Fat 75%
Protein 19%
Carbs 6%

Per Serving
Calories: 674
Total fat: 56g
Protein: 31g
Total carbs: 14g
Fiber: 4g
Net carbs: 10g
Sodium: 1,216mg
Cholesterol: 62mg

Thai Red Curry Beef with Coconut Milk

Serves 6 to 8 • Prep: 15 minutes • Cook: 8 hours on low

This is a quick and easy way to make a delicious, sweet-spicy Thai-style beef curry. You can buy curry paste in the international aisle of most supermarkets; the brands vary quite a bit in spice level. Start with a little and add more to suit your personal taste.

4 tablespoons coconut oil, divided

1 (1¼-pound) beef chuck roast

Kosher salt

Freshly ground black pepper

1 onion, diced

1 to 2 tablespoons Thai red curry paste

2 teaspoons ground cumin

1 teaspoon ground coriander

2 cups chicken or beef broth

1 (14-ounce) can coconut milk

½ cup all-natural peanut butter

3 tablespoons fish sauce

Juice of 1 lime

1 teaspoon blackstrap molasses

4 garlic cloves, minced

1 (3-inch) piece fresh ginger, peeled and sliced

2 teaspoons stevia powder

2 bay leaves

¼ cup chopped roasted peanuts

¼ cup chopped fresh cilantro

1. In a large skillet, heat 2 tablespoons of coconut oil over medium-high heat.

2. Generously season the beef with salt and pepper. Place the roast in the skillet and cook until browned on all sides, about 6 minutes.

3. In the slow cooker, toss the onion with the remaining 2 tablespoons of coconut oil and spread to cover the insert bottom. Place the browned meat on top.

4. Add the curry paste, cumin, and coriander to the hot skillet. Cook, stirring, for about 30 seconds. Stir in the broth and bring to a boil.

5. Stir in the coconut milk, peanut butter, fish sauce, lime juice, molasses, garlic, ginger, stevia, and bay leaves. Bring to a boil. Pour the mixture over the meat in the slow cooker. Cover and cook for 8 hours on low.

6. Using two forks, shred the meat in the cooker and stir into the sauce. Discard the bay leaves and serve hot, garnished with peanuts and cilantro.

Make It Paleo Substitute almond butter for the peanut butter and chopped toasted almonds for the chopped peanuts.

Ginger Curry Beef

Serves 6 • Prep: 10 minutes • Cook: 8 hours on low

QUICK PREP
ALLERGEN-FREE
PALEO FRIENDLY

This ginger curry gets unique flavor from a custom blend of spices, but you can also substitute 3 tablespoons curry powder for all the spices listed. As with most curries, this dish turns out saucy, so it's great served over cauliflower rice.

1 cup diced tomatoes

1 (14-ounce) can coconut milk

⅓ cup water

¼ cup coconut oil, melted

¼ cup tomato paste

1 onion, diced

6 garlic cloves, minced

3 tablespoons grated fresh ginger

2 tablespoons ground cumin

1 teaspoon paprika

1 teaspoon kosher salt

½ teaspoon ground turmeric

½ teaspoon ground cardamom

½ teaspoon ground cinnamon

½ teaspoon ground cloves

½ teaspoon cayenne pepper

¼ teaspoon ground nutmeg

1 (1½-pound) beef chuck roast, cut into ½-by-2-inch strips

⅓ cup chopped fresh cilantro

Macronutrients
Fat 75%
Protein 20%
Carbs 5%

Per Serving
Calories: 547
Total fat: 46g
Protein: 26g
Total carbs: 12g
Fiber: 3g
Net carbs: 9g
Sodium: 486mg
Cholesterol: 75mg

1. In the slow cooker, stir together the tomatoes, coconut milk, water, coconut oil, and tomato paste.

2. Add the onion, garlic, ginger, cumin, paprika, salt, turmeric, cardamom, cinnamon, cloves, cayenne, and nutmeg.

3. Add the beef and toss to mix well. Cover and cook for 8 hours on low. Serve hot, garnished with the cilantro.

Variation Tip Add 2 cups cauliflower or broccoli florets about 30 minutes before the end of the cooking time.

Macronutrients
Fat 70%
Protein 26%
Carbs 4%

Per Serving
Calories: 675
Total fat: 52g
Protein: 47g
Total carbs: 7g
Fiber: 2g
Net carbs: 5g
Sodium: 1,131mg
Cholesterol: 198mg

Steak Roulades with Feta Cheese, Spinach & Olives

Serves 4 • Prep: 15 minutes • Cook: 6 hours on low or 3 hours on high

Rolling steak around a flavorful filling of spinach and feta cheese makes for an elegant presentation, but the dish is still ultra-quick and easy to make. Serve buttered zucchini noodles and a side salad to round out the meal.

4 (5-ounce) pieces skirt steak, pounded to ½-inch thickness

½ teaspoon kosher salt

½ teaspoon freshly ground black pepper

4 cups chopped baby spinach

1 small onion, diced

1 cup grated Parmesan cheese

4 ounces feta cheese, crumbled

½ cup chopped Kalamata olives

¼ cup beef broth or water

5 tablespoons unsalted butter or Ghee (page 179)

1 cup heavy (whipping) cream

1. Season the steak all over with the salt and pepper.

2. In a medium bowl, mix the spinach, onion, Parmesan, feta, and olives. Top each steak with one-quarter of the mixture, placing it close to one of the short sides. Starting with the short side closest to the filling, roll the steaks around the filling. Use wooden toothpicks or kitchen twine, if needed, to secure the rolls. Arrange the rolls in a single layer in the slow cooker.

3. Pour in the beef broth. Cover and cook for 6 hours on low or 3 hours on high. When finished, remove the roulades from the slow cooker and let them rest for a few minutes.

4. While the roulades are resting, add the butter and heavy cream to the slow cooker and stir to melt the butter and mix well with the cooking juices.

5. Slice the roulades into pinwheels and serve hot, with the cream sauce spooned over the top.

Variation Tip For added flavor, dice 4 bacon slices and fry them in a hot skillet until crisp, then add it to the filling mixture.

Short Ribs Braised in Coconut Milk with Chili Paste

Serves 6 • Prep: 10 minutes • Cook: 9 hours on low or 4 ½ hours on high

These spicy braised short ribs are succulent and meaty. If you buy your short ribs from a butcher, ask for them to be cut into 3-inch lengths, if possible, to make it easier to fit them in your slow cooker and to serve.

1 onion, diced

3 garlic cloves, minced

1 tablespoon minced fresh ginger

1 (14-ounce) can coconut milk

2 tablespoons soy sauce, tamari, or coconut aminos

2 tablespoons mirin

2 tablespoons toasted sesame oil

2 teaspoons blackstrap molasses

1 teaspoon or less chili paste for seasoning

1 teaspoon stevia powder

1 pound short ribs

3 scallions, thinly sliced

¼ cup toasted sesame seeds

Macronutrients
Fat 80%
Protein 13%
Carbs 7%

Per Serving
Calories: 553
Total fat: 50g
Protein: 16g
Total carbs: 12g
Fiber: 3g
Net carbs: 9g
Sodium: 435mg
Cholesterol: 57mg

1. In the slow cooker, stir together the onion, garlic, ginger, coconut milk, soy sauce, mirin, sesame oil, molasses, chili paste, and stevia powder.

2. Add the short ribs and stir to coat them well. Cover and cook for 9 hours on low or 4 ½ hours on high. Serve hot, garnished with the scallions and sesame seeds.

Variation Tip For even more flavor, the night before cooking, complete step 1 in a large bowl instead of the slow cooker insert and then add the ribs and stir to coat. Cover and refrigerate overnight. Remove the ingredients from the refrigerator 30 to 60 minutes before cooking to let them come to room temperature. Alternatively, you could set a timer to turn the slow cooker on 60 minutes after you put the refrigerated ingredients in the pot.

BEEF & LAMB DISHES

Macronutrients
Fat 69%
Protein 25%
Carbs 6%

Per Serving
Calories: 747
Total fat: 56g
Protein: 47g
Total carbs: 9g
Fiber: 3g
Net carbs: 6g
Sodium: 1,084mg
Cholesterol: 224mg

North African Braised Beef

Serves 4 to 6 • Prep: 10 minutes • Cook: 9 hours on low or 4 ½ hours on high

North African cuisine is marked by a layering of flavors from heady spices to sweet fruits, fresh herbs, and toasted nuts. This braised beef dish starts with cumin, cinnamon, and ginger for warm spice, then adds orange juice and zest for a sweet fruitiness, and is topped with toasted almond slices and cilantro.

¼ cup coconut oil

1 medium onion, diced

2 teaspoons ground cumin

1 ½ teaspoons kosher salt

½ teaspoon freshly ground black pepper

½ teaspoon ground cinnamon

½ teaspoon ground ginger

1 cup dry red wine

1 (1 ¼-pound) beef chuck roast, cut into 2-inch pieces

Grated zest and juice of 1 orange

1 cup heavy (whipping) cream

5 tablespoons unsalted butter

½ cup ground toasted almonds

¼ cup chopped fresh cilantro

1. In a large skillet, heat the coconut oil over medium-high heat. Add the onion and sauté until soft, about 5 minutes.

2. Add the cumin, salt, pepper, cinnamon, and ginger. Sauté for 1 minute more.

3. Stir in the red wine and bring to a boil. Cook for 1 to 2 minutes, scraping up any browned bits from the bottom of the pan. Transfer the mixture to the slow cooker.

4. Stir in the beef, orange zest, and orange juice. Cover and cook for 9 hours on low or 4 ½ hours on high.

5. Stir in the heavy cream and butter until the butter melts and both are well incorporated. Serve hot, garnished with the almonds and cilantro.

Make It Allergen-Free Substitute additional coconut oil for the butter, full-fat coconut milk for the heavy cream, and toasted pumpkin seeds for the almonds.

Greek Lamb & Eggplant Casserole (Moussaka)

Serves 6 • Prep: 15 minutes • Cook: 8 hours on low

This rich casserole delivers a distinctively Greek combination of ingredients. Lamb, nutmeg, cinnamon, oregano, garlic, and eggplant are slow cooked in a creamy béchamel-style sauce flavored with feta cheese to make a delicious and satisfying meal. I promise, your guests will be surprised to learn that this dish took only 15 minutes of prep time.

1 large eggplant, peeled and cut into ¼-inch-thick slices

1¼ pounds ground lamb

1 (14.5-ounce) can diced tomatoes, drained

1 cup tomato sauce

1 onion, diced

5 garlic cloves, minced

1 teaspoon dried oregano

1 teaspoon kosher salt

1 teaspoon freshly ground black pepper

½ teaspoon ground nutmeg

½ teaspoon ground cinnamon

1 cup heavy (whipping) cream

3 large egg yolks

¾ cup feta cheese

2 tablespoons minced fresh parsley

1. In the bottom of the slow cooker, arrange half of the eggplant slices. They should cover the bottom completely, overlapping as necessary.

2. In a large skillet, sauté the lamb over medium-high heat until browned, about 5 minutes. With a slotted spoon, transfer the meat to a large bowl, leaving any excess fat behind in the skillet.

3. Add the tomatoes, tomato sauce, onion, garlic, oregano, salt, pepper, nutmeg, and cinnamon to the lamb. Stir to mix well. Spread the meat mixture over the eggplant slices in the slow cooker and arrange the remaining eggplant slices over the top.

4. In a medium bowl, whisk together the heavy cream, egg yolks, and feta cheese. Pour this over the ingredients in the slow cooker. Cover and cook for 8 hours on low. Serve hot, garnished with the parsley.

Make It Allergen-Free/Paleo Omit the sauce of heavy cream, egg yolks, and feta cheese.

Macronutrients
Fat 73%
Protein 18%
Carbs 9%

Per Serving
Calories: 730
Total fat: 61g
Protein: 30g
Total carbs: 17g
Fiber: 4g
Net carbs: 13g
Sodium: 735mg
Cholesterol: 259mg

BEEF & LAMB DISHES

Macronutrients

Fat 75%

Protein 20%

Carbs 5%

Per Serving
Calories: 512
Total fat: 44g
Protein: 25g
Total carbs: 6g
Fiber: 2g
Net carbs: 4g
Sodium: 465mg
Cholesterol: 76mg

Lamb Curry

Serves 6 · Prep: 10 minutes · Cook: 8 hours on low or 4 hours on high

Since curry powder is a mix of numerous spices, you get a whole lot of flavor out of one simple ingredient. Each curry powder is a bit different, so try various brands, if possible, to find one you love. Curry leaves are a common component of South Indian cooking. These small, shiny leaves have a pungent smell and flavor reminiscent of curry powder (though the two are unrelated). You can buy curry leaves fresh or frozen at Indian or Asian markets, or find them online. You can also substitute cilantro—the flavor will be different, but just as delicious. Serve this saucy curry over cauliflower rice, if desired.

1½ pounds lamb stew meat, cut into 1½-inch cubes

1 onion, diced

2 garlic cloves, minced

1 tablespoon grated fresh ginger

1 tablespoon curry powder

1 teaspoon kosher salt

¾ teaspoon freshly ground black pepper

½ teaspoon cayenne pepper

1 (14-ounce) can coconut milk

¼ cup coconut oil, melted

½ cup ground toasted almonds (optional)

8 to 10 whole curry leaves or ½ cup chopped fresh cilantro

1. In the slow cooker, combine the lamb, onion, garlic, ginger, curry powder, salt, black pepper, and cayenne pepper.

2. Add the coconut milk and coconut oil and stir to mix. Cover and cook for 8 hours on low or 4 hours on high.

3. Serve hot, garnished with the ground almonds (if using) and curry leaves.

Variation Tip You can also make this with (70% lean) ground beef. It should be browned in a skillet on the stove top before adding to the slow cooker, but the dish cooks more quickly once in the cooker. Cook for 5 hours on low or 2½ hours on high.

Braised Lamb with Fennel

Serves 4 • Prep: 15 minutes • Cook: 8 hours on low

Lamb shanks become fall-off-the-bone tender in the slow cooker. Here they're flavored with onions, fresh fennel, tomatoes, wine, and a bit of orange juice. Serve zucchini noodles or spaghetti squash alongside to soak up the delicious sauce.

1½ pounds lamb stew meat, cut into 2-inch pieces

1 teaspoon kosher salt

½ teaspoon freshly ground black pepper

¼ cup (½ stick) unsalted butter, Ghee (page 179), or coconut oil

1 onion, sliced

1 cup sliced fennel

1 (14.5-ounce) can diced tomatoes, drained

½ cup dry red wine

2 tablespoons tomato paste

2 garlic cloves, minced

2 teaspoons paprika

Pinch stevia powder

1 cinnamon stick

1 cup heavy (whipping) cream

¾ cup chopped pistachios

2 tablespoons chopped fresh mint

1. Season the lamb with the salt and pepper.

2. In a large skillet, heat the butter over medium-high heat. Add the lamb and cook until browned on all sides, about 8 minutes. Transfer the meat to the slow cooker.

3. Return the skillet to medium-high heat and add the onion and fennel. Sauté until softened, about 3 minutes.

4. Stir in the tomatoes, red wine, tomato paste, garlic, paprika, stevia, and cinnamon. Bring to a boil. Transfer the sauce to the cooker. Cover and cook for 8 hours on low.

5. Just before serving, discard the cinnamon stick and stir in the heavy cream. Serve hot, garnished with the pistachios and mint.

Variation Tip For an additional layer of flavor, add 1 cup halved Kalamata olives to the slow cooker 30 minutes before the end of the cooking time.

QUICK PREP

Macronutrients
Fat 75%
Protein 17%
Carbs 8%

Per Serving
Calories: 686
Total fat: 60g
Protein: 28g
Total carbs: 13g
Fiber: 3g
Net carbs: 10g
Sodium: 498mg
Cholesterol: 130mg

SEVEN

Desserts & Sweet Treats

Macronutrients
Fat 75%
Protein 12%
Carbs 13%

Per Serving
Calories: 275
Total fat: 23g
Protein: 8g
Total carbs: 9g
Fiber: 5g
Net carbs: 4g
Sodium: 32mg
Cholesterol: 0mg

Cinnamon-Cocoa Almonds

Serves 8 • Prep: 5 minutes • Cook: 2 hours on high

These spicy-sweet almonds make a really satisfying mid-afternoon snack. They cook in just 2 hours, and need to be stirred every 30 minutes during that time, but you can make a big batch (double the recipe, if you like). They'll last a long time in your pantry and come in handy as a great ready-made snack when you need something you can grab on the run.

3 cups raw almonds

3 tablespoons coconut oil, melted

Kosher salt

¼ cup erythritol

1 tablespoon unsweetened cocoa powder

1 tablespoon ground cinnamon

1. In the slow cooker, stir together the almonds and coconut oil until the nuts are well coated. Season with salt.

2. Mix in the erythritol, cocoa powder, and cinnamon. Cover and cook for 2 hours on high, stirring every 30 minutes.

3. Transfer the nuts to a large, rimmed baking sheet and spread them out to cool quickly. Serve immediately or store in a covered container for up to 3 weeks.

Make It Paleo Simply leave out the sweetener, or replace it with a paleo-friendly sweetener, such as coconut sugar.

Coconut Custard

Serves 8 • Prep: 5 minutes • Cook: 5 hours on low, plus 1 to 2 hours to cool

This easy custard couldn't be simpler. Coconut milk and eggs, a bit of sweetener, and a shot of coconut extract are all you need to make it. Set your timer so it cooks for 5 hours and then shuts off. It can cool in the slow cooker for another hour or two.

1 tablespoon coconut oil

8 large eggs, lightly beaten

4 cups canned coconut milk

1 cup erythritol or 1 teaspoon stevia powder

2 teaspoons stevia powder

1 teaspoon coconut extract

1. Generously coat the inside of the slow cooker insert with the coconut oil.

2. In the insert, stir together the eggs, coconut milk, erythritol, stevia powder, and coconut extract until well combined.

3. Cover and cook for 5 hours on low. Turn off the cooker and let cool in the slow cooker for 1 to 2 hours.

4. Serve immediately or refrigerate for up to 3 days and serve chilled.

Variation Tip You can easily change the flavor of this custard. Instead of coconut milk and extract, try heavy cream and 1 tablespoon vanilla bean paste for a simple vanilla custard. Alternatively, you could add ½ cup sugar-free chocolate chips to the filling.

Macronutrients
Fat 84%
Protein 9%
Carbs 7%

Per Serving
Calories: 375
Total fat: 35g
Protein: 8g
Total carbs: 7g
Fiber: 3g
Net carbs: 4g
Sodium: 80mg
Cholesterol: 164mg

Macronutrients

Fat 84%

Protein 9%

Carbs 7%

Per Serving

Calories: 375

Total fat: 35g

Protein: 8g

Total carbs: 7g

Fiber: 3g

Net carbs: 4g

Sodium: 80mg

Cholesterol: 164mg

Spicy Chai Custard

Serves 8 • Prep: 10 minutes • Cook: 5 hours on low, plus 1 to 2 hours to cool

Chai is a delicious blend of black tea and Indian spices, such as cardamom, cinnamon, ginger, and peppercorns, steeped in milk and sweetened with sugar. Steeping chai tea bags in coconut milk and then cooking the flavored coconut milk into an egg-based custard sweetened with erythritol makes a rich, dairy-free, sugar-free dessert that's irresistible.

4 cups canned coconut milk

4 chai tea bags

1 tablespoon coconut oil

8 large eggs, lightly beaten

1 cup erythritol or 1 teaspoon stevia powder

2 teaspoons stevia powder

1 teaspoon pure vanilla extract or vanilla bean paste

1. In a medium saucepan, heat the coconut milk over medium-high heat until it simmers. Remove from the heat and add the tea bags. Steep for 5 to 10 minutes. Remove and discard the tea bags.

2. Generously coat the inside of the slow cooker insert with the coconut oil.

3. In the insert, stir together the tea-infused coconut milk, eggs, erythritol, stevia powder, and vanilla until well combined. Cover and cook for 5 hours on low. Turn off the cooker and let cool in the slow cooker for 1 to 2 hours.

4. Serve immediately or refrigerate for up to 3 days and serve chilled.

Variation Tip If you want to skip the infusing step, omit the tea bags and replace 1 cup of the coconut milk with 1 cup of sugar-free chai tea concentrate.

Pumpkin Spice Pudding

Serves 10 • Prep: 5 minutes • Cook: 8 hours on low

This easy pudding is essentially a crustless pumpkin pie that's low carb, grain free, and dairy free. Serve it topped with lightly sweetened whipped coconut cream for a festive low-carb dessert on Thanksgiving, or any other time you're in the mood for a little pumpkin spice.

3 tablespoons melted coconut oil, plus more for coating the slow cooker insert

2 cups canned coconut milk

1½ cups puréed pumpkin

4 large eggs, lightly beaten

1 tablespoon pure vanilla extract

½ cup erythritol

¼ cup almond flour

2 teaspoons pumpkin pie spice

1 teaspoon stevia powder

1 teaspoon baking powder

Macronutrients
Fat 79%
Protein 8%
Carbs 13%

Per Serving
Calories: 215
Total fat: 19g
Protein: 4g
Total carbs: 7g
Fiber: 3g
Net carbs: 4g
Sodium: 34mg
Cholesterol: 65mg

1. Generously coat the inside of the slow cooker insert with coconut oil.

2. In the insert, stir together 3 tablespoons of coconut oil, coconut milk, pumpkin, eggs, vanilla, erythritol, almond flour, pumpkin pie spice, stevia powder, and baking powder until smooth. Cover and cook for 8 hours on low.

3. Serve warm or refrigerate for up to 3 days and serve chilled.

Variation Tip Make this into a pumpkin cream pie by adding a crust made of 1 cup ground nuts, 1 tablespoon coconut oil, 1 egg, and 1 teaspoon stevia powder. Press the crust into the slow cooker before adding the filling. Serve it topped with sweetened whipped cream or whipped coconut cream.

Macronutrients
Fat 77%
Protein 9%
Carbs 14%

Per Serving
Calories: 223
Total fat: 19g
Protein: 5g
Total carbs: 8g
Fiber: 3g
Net carbs: 5g
Sodium: 35mg
Cholesterol: 65mg

Chocolate & Coconut Pudding

Serves 10 • Prep: 10 minutes • Cook: 8 hours on low

This rich, dark chocolate pudding laced with nutty coconut tastes just like one of my favorite candy bars from childhood. Serve it topped with a dollop of lightly sweetened whipped cream or whipped coconut cream, if you like.

3 tablespoons melted coconut oil, plus more for coating the slow cooker insert

4 ounces unsweetened chocolate, chopped

2 cups canned coconut milk

4 large eggs, lightly beaten

2 teaspoons coconut extract

1 teaspoon pure vanilla extract

½ cup erythritol

¼ cup almond flour

1 teaspoon stevia powder

1 teaspoon baking powder

1. Generously coat the inside of the slow cooker insert with coconut oil.

2. In a microwave-safe bowl or measuring cup, combine 3 tablespoons of coconut oil with the chocolate. Microwave for 1 minute on high. Stir, and then microwave in 30-second intervals, stirring in between, until the chocolate is melted and smooth. Transfer to the prepared insert.

3. Stir in the coconut milk, eggs, coconut and vanilla extracts, erythritol, almond flour, stevia powder, and baking powder until smooth. Cover and cook for 8 hours on low. Serve warm or refrigerate for up to 3 days and serve chilled.

Variation Tip Make this into a luscious chocolate cream pie by adding a crust made of 1 cup ground macadamia nuts or hazelnuts, 1 tablespoon coconut oil, 1 egg, and 1 teaspoon stevia powder. Press the crust into the slow cooker before adding the filling. Top with whipped cream or whipped coconut cream, if desired.

Coconut-Raspberry Cake

Serves 10 • Prep: 10 minutes • Cook: 3 hours, plus 3 to 4 hours to cool

QUICK PREP
PALEO FRIENDLY

Macronutrients
Fat 80%
Protein 10%
Carbs 10%

Per Serving
Calories: 405
Total fat: 38g
Protein: 11g
Total carbs: 10g
Fiber: 5g
Net carbs: 5g
Sodium: 358mg
Cholesterol: 127mg

This simple grain-free, dairy-free cake is studded with raspberries and shredded coconut and delivers intense coconut flavor. It cooks for only 3 hours in the slow cooker, but you can set your timer to shut the cooker off at the 3-hour mark and let the cake sit in the slow cooker for another 3 to 4 hours to cool. Serve it dolloped with lightly sweetened coconut whipped cream for an extra-special treat.

½ cup melted coconut oil, plus more for coating the slow cooker insert

2 cups almond flour

1 cup unsweetened shredded coconut

1 cup erythritol or 1 teaspoon stevia powder

¼ cup unsweetened, unflavored protein powder

2 teaspoons baking soda

¼ teaspoon fine sea salt

4 large eggs, lightly beaten

¾ cup canned coconut milk

1 teaspoon coconut extract

1 cup raspberries, fresh or frozen

1. Generously coat the inside of the slow cooker insert with coconut oil.

2. In a large bowl, stir together the almond flour, coconut, erythritol, protein powder, baking soda, and sea salt.

3. Whisk in the eggs, coconut milk, ½ cup of coconut oil, and coconut extract.

4. Gently fold in the raspberries.

5. Transfer the batter to the prepared slow cooker, cover, and cook for 3 hours on low. Turn off the slow cooker and let the cake cool for several hours, to room temperature. Serve at room temperature.

Variation Tip Use blueberries instead of raspberries, depending on your tastes and what's on hand. Or, for a bigger change, substitute sugar-free chocolate chips for the berries.

Macronutrients

Fat 82%

Protein 9%

Carbs 9%

Per Serving

Calories: 420

Total fat: 40g

Protein: 11g

Total carbs: 10g

Fiber: 4g

Net carbs: 6g

Sodium: 45mg

Cholesterol: 137mg

Tangy Lemon Cake
with Lemon Glaze

Serves 8 • Prep: 10 minutes • Cook: 6 hours on low or 3 hours on high

This tangy lemon cake is both rich and refreshing. Serve it with a dollop of lightly sweetened whipped cream or whipped coconut cream and top it with a few fresh blueberries or raspberries, if you like.

FOR THE GLAZE

½ cup boiling water

¼ cup erythritol

2 tablespoons unsalted butter or Ghee (page 179), melted

2 tablespoons freshly squeezed lemon juice

FOR THE CAKE

Coconut oil, for coating the insert

2 cups almond flour

½ cup erythritol

2 teaspoons baking powder

3 large eggs

½ cup (1 stick) unsalted butter or Ghee (page 179), melted and cooled slightly

½ cup heavy (whipping) cream

Grated zest and juice of 2 lemons

TO MAKE THE GLAZE

In a small bowl, stir together all the ingredients. Set aside.

TO MAKE THE CAKE

1. Coat the inside of the slow cooker insert with coconut oil.

2. In a medium bowl, mix the almond flour, erythritol, and baking powder.

3. In a large bowl, beat the eggs, then whisk in the butter, heavy cream, lemon zest, and lemon juice.

4. Add the dry ingredients to the wet ingredients. Stir to mix well. Transfer the batter to the insert and spread evenly with a rubber spatula.

5. Pour the glaze over the cake batter. Cover and cook for 6 hours on low or 3 hours on high. Serve warm or at room temperature.

Variation Tip For a slightly different taste, fold 1 cup fresh blueberries into the batter just before transferring it to the slow cooker.

Moist Ginger Cake
with Whipped Cream

Serves 10 • Prep: 15 minutes • Cook: 3 hours on low

QUICK PREP
PALEO FRIENDLY

Macronutrients
Fat 80%
Protein 10%
Carbs 10%

Per Serving
Calories: 453
Total fat: 43g
Protein: 12g
Total carbs: 12g
Fiber: 5g
Net carbs: 7g
Sodium: 103mg
Cholesterol: 109mg

This rich, spicy cake takes only 3 hours to cook, which is good since your house will smell so amazing while it's cooking, you won't want to wait to dig in. Better still, it makes 10 servings, so you can make it on a Sunday and enjoy this dessert all week.

FOR THE CAKE

½ cup (1 stick) unsalted butter, melted, plus more for coating the slow cooker insert

2¼ cups almond flour

¾ cup erythritol

2 tablespoons coconut flour

1½ tablespoons ground ginger

1 tablespoon unsweetened cocoa powder

2 teaspoons baking powder

1½ teaspoons ground cinnamon

½ teaspoon ground cloves

¼ teaspoon fine sea salt

4 large eggs, lightly beaten

⅔ cup heavy (whipping) cream

1 teaspoon pure vanilla extract

FOR THE WHIPPED CREAM

1 cup heavy (whipping) cream

½ teaspoon stevia powder
or ½ cup erythritol

1 teaspoon pure vanilla extract

TO MAKE THE CAKE

1. Generously coat the inside of the slow cooker insert with butter.

2. In a large bowl, mix the almond flour, erythritol, coconut flour, ginger, cocoa powder, baking powder, cinnamon, cloves, and sea salt.

3. Add butter, eggs, heavy cream, and vanilla. Mix and transfer to the insert.

4. Cover and cook for 3 hours on low. Serve warm with whipped cream.

TO MAKE THE WHIPPED CREAM

In a large bowl, use an electric mixer set on medium-high to beat the heavy cream, stevia, and vanilla until stiff peaks form, about 5 minutes.

Chocolate–Macadamia Nut Cheesecake

Serves 8 • Prep: 15 minutes • Cook: 4 hours on low or 2 hours on high, plus time to chill

This rich, chocolaty cheesecake is beyond divine. The macadamia nuts in both the crust and topping add heart-healthy monounsaturated fat and omega-3 fatty acids, both of which help you lose weight. Macadamia nuts are also a source of palmitoleic acid, a monounsaturated fatty acid that may help boost fat metabolism.

FOR THE CRUST

1 cup macadamia nuts, ground to a meal

1 large egg, lightly beaten

2 tablespoons coconut oil, melted

1 teaspoon stevia powder

1 cup water

TO MAKE THE CRUST

1. In a medium bowl, stir together the macadamia nut meal, egg, coconut oil, and stevia powder. Press the mixture into the bottom of a baking pan that fits into your slow cooker (make sure there is room on the sides so you can lift the pan out). An oval baking dish, round cake pan, or loaf pan could all work, depending on the size and shape of your slow cooker.

2. Pour the water into the slow cooker insert. Place the pan in the cooker.

Variation Tip Top this rich cheesecake with lightly sweetened whipped cream or whipped coconut cream—simply whip 1 cup heavy (whipping) cream or coconut cream with 2 tablespoons erythritol and ½ teaspoon pure vanilla extract.

FOR THE FILLING

6 ounces unsweetened chocolate, chopped

2 large eggs

2 (8-ounce) packages cream cheese, at room temperature

¼ cup coconut cream

1 tablespoon coconut flour

1 teaspoon pure vanilla extract

½ cup erythritol

½ teaspoon stevia powder

¼ cup coarsely chopped macadamia nuts

TO MAKE THE FILLING

1. In a microwave-safe bowl, heat the chocolate in the microwave for 1 minute on high. Stir and then microwave in 30-second intervals, stirring in between, until the chocolate is melted and smooth. Set aside.

2. In a large bowl, beat the eggs, then beat in the cream cheese, coconut cream, coconut flour, vanilla, erythritol, and stevia powder.

3. Stir in the chocolate until well incorporated. Pour the mixture over the crust. Cover and cook for 4 hours on low or 2 hours on high.

4. When finished, turn off the slow cooker and let the cheesecake sit inside until cooled to room temperature, up to 3 hours.

5. Remove the pan from the slow cooker and refrigerate until chilled, about 2 hours more.

6. Sprinkle the macadamia nuts over the top and serve chilled.

Macronutrients
Fat 86%
Protein 9%
Carbs 5%

Per Serving
Calories: 338
Total fat: 33g
Protein: 7g
Total carbs: 5g
Fiber: 1g
Net carbs: 4g
Sodium: 208mg
Cholesterol: 146mg

Vanilla Cheesecake

Serves 8 • Prep: 15 minutes • Cook: 4 hours on low or 2 hours on high, plus time to chill

Toasted walnuts make a crunchy, flavorful crust for this creamy low-carb vanilla cheesecake. If you set the timer to shut the cooker off when done, it can sit for 2 or 3 hours while it cools. Serve it on its own or topped with fresh berries, if you like.

FOR THE CRUST

1 cup toasted walnuts, ground to a meal

1 large egg, lightly beaten

2 tablespoons coconut oil, melted

1 teaspoon stevia powder

1 cup water

FOR THE FILLING

2 large eggs

2 (8-ounce) packages cream cheese, at room temperature

¼ cup heavy (whipping) cream

2 teaspoons pure vanilla extract

½ cup erythritol

1 tablespoon coconut flour

½ teaspoon stevia powder

TO MAKE THE CRUST

1. In a medium bowl, mix the walnut meal, egg, coconut oil, and stevia powder. Press the mixture into the bottom of a baking pan that fits into your slow cooker (make sure there is room to lift the pan out). An oval baking dish, round cake pan, or loaf pan could all work, depending on the size and shape of your slow cooker.

2. Pour the water into the slow cooker insert. Place the pan in the cooker.

TO MAKE THE FILLING

1. In a large bowl, beat the eggs, then beat in the cream cheese, heavy cream, vanilla, erythritol, coconut flour, and stevia powder. Pour the mixture over the crust. Cover and cook for 4 hours on low or 2 hours on high.

2. When finished, turn off the cooker and let the cheesecake sit inside until cooled to room temperature, up to 3 hours.

3. Remove the pan from the slow cooker and refrigerate until chilled, about 2 hours more. Serve chilled.

Variation Tip Experiment by adding the zest and juice of 1 lemon to the filling and reducing the vanilla to 1 teaspoon.

Toasted Almond Cheesecake

Serves 8 • Prep: 15 minutes • Cook: 4 hours on low or 2 hours on high, plus time to chill

QUICK PREP

FASTER COOK
OPTION

This slow cooker cheesecake builds on toasted almond flavor. Ground, toasted almonds, almond butter, and almond extract give it a triple punch of nuttiness.

Macronutrients
Fat 82%
Protein 9%
Carbs 9%

FOR THE CRUST

1 cup toasted almonds,
ground to a meal

1 large egg, lightly beaten

2 tablespoons coconut oil,
melted

1 teaspoon stevia powder

1 cup water

FOR THE FILLING

2 large eggs

2 (8-ounce) packages cream cheese,
at room temperature

¾ cup almond butter

¼ cup coconut cream

1 teaspoon pure almond extract

¾ cup erythritol

1 tablespoon coconut flour

2 teaspoons stevia powder

Per Serving
Calories: 538
Total fat: 51g
Protein: 14g
Total carbs: 12g
Fiber: 3g
Net carbs: 9g
Sodium: 215mg
Cholesterol: 141mg

TO MAKE THE CRUST

1. In a medium bowl, mix the almond meal, egg, coconut oil, and stevia powder. Press the mixture into the bottom of a baking pan that fits into your slow cooker (make sure there is room to lift the pan out). Many pans could work, depending on the size and shape of your slow cooker.

2. Pour the water into the slow cooker insert. Place the pan in the cooker.

TO MAKE THE FILLING

1. In a large bowl, beat the eggs, then beat in the cream cheese, almond butter, coconut cream, almond extract, erythritol, coconut flour, and stevia powder. Pour the mixture over the crust. Cover and cook for 4 hours on low or 2 hours on high.

2. When finished, turn off the slow cooker and let the cheesecake sit inside until cooled to room temperature, up to 3 hours.

3. Remove the pan from the slow cooker and refrigerate until chilled, about 2 hours more. Serve chilled.

Variation Tip Substitute peanuts and peanut butter for the almonds and almond butter.

Macronutrients

Fat 83%

Protein 8%

Carbs 9%

Per Serving
Calories: 234
Total fat: 23g
Protein: 6g
Total carbs: 8g
Fiber: 4g
Net carbs: 4g
Sodium: 131mg
Cholesterol: 21mg

Chocolate Chip Cookies

Serves 10 • Prep: 10 minutes • Cook: 2 ½ hours on low

When you are craving a sweet treat in the middle of the afternoon, few things are as welcome as a chocolate chip cookie. This low-carb, grain-free version is studded with sugar-free chocolate chunks. Look for an all-natural brand of sugar-free chocolate chunks or chips or buy an all-natural sugar-free chocolate bar that you like and chop it yourself.

¼ cup coconut oil, melted, plus more for coating the parchment

1 cup erythritol

1 teaspoon stevia powder

1 egg, beaten

½ teaspoon pure vanilla extract

1½ cups almond flour

1¾ teaspoons baking powder

½ teaspoon fine sea salt

4 ounces unsweetened chocolate, chopped

½ cup chopped toasted walnuts

1. Line a slow cooker insert with enough parchment or wax paper to extend over the sides slightly. Coat the parchment with coconut oil.

2. In a large bowl, stir together the ¼ cup of melted coconut oil, erythritol, and stevia powder.

3. Beat in the egg and vanilla.

4. Add the almond flour, baking powder, and sea salt and beat until well combined.

5. Gently fold in the chocolate and walnuts.

6. Transfer the dough to the prepared insert and press it into an even layer, covering the bottom of the insert. Cover and cook for 2 ½ hours on low. Using the parchment as a sling, lift the cookie out of the insert and transfer to a wire rack to cool. Cut into squares and serve warm or at room temperature.

Variation Tip Make this cookie even more special by leaving the chocolate out of the cookies. After the cookie has cooled, combine the chocolate with 1 tablespoon coconut oil and microwave on high for 30-second intervals, stirring in between, until the chocolate is melted. Stir to combine well. Pour the chocolate mixture over the cooked cookie. Refrigerate until the chocolate sets, about 30 minutes. Slice and serve.

Chocolate Walnut Fudge

Serves 12 • Prep: 15 minutes • Cook: 2 hours on low, plus 3 hours to cool, overnight to chill

QUICK PREP

MAKE IT
ALLERGEN-FREE

PALEO FRIENDLY

WORTH THE
EFFORT

This rich, creamy fudge requires a few steps, so it is best made on a day when you can check it every few hours. The good news is that it makes a large amount and will keep in the refrigerator for a couple of weeks. Oh, and also that it is a rich, creamy, chocolaty fudge that is also low carb and free of grains, sugar, and dairy.

Coconut oil, for coating the slow cooker insert and a baking dish

1 cup canned coconut milk

4 ounces unsweetened chocolate, chopped

1 cup erythritol

2 teaspoons stevia powder

¼ teaspoon fine sea salt

2 teaspoons pure vanilla extract

1 cup chopped toasted walnuts

Macronutrients
Fat 87%
Protein 6%
Carbs 7%

Per Serving
Calories: 128
Total fat: 13g
Protein: 3g
Total carbs: 4g
Fiber: 2g
Net carbs: 2g
Sodium: 53mg
Cholesterol: 0mg

1. Generously coat the inside of the slow cooker insert with coconut oil.

2. In a large bowl, whisk the coconut milk into a uniform consistency. Add the chocolate, erythritol, stevia powder, and sea salt. Stir to mix well. Pour into the slow cooker. Cover and cook for 2 hours on low.

3. When finished, stir in the vanilla.

4. Let the fudge sit in the slow cooker, with the lid off, until it cools to room temperature, about 3 hours.

5. Coat a large baking dish with coconut oil and set aside.

6. Stir the fudge until it becomes glossy, about 10 minutes.

7. Stir in the walnuts. Transfer the mixture to the prepared baking dish and smooth it into an even layer with a rubber spatula. Refrigerate overnight. Serve chilled, cut into small pieces.

Make It Allergen-Free/Paleo Omit the walnuts to make it allergen-free. Substitute coconut sugar for the erythritol and vanilla bean paste for the vanilla extract to make it paleo friendly.

Per Serving

Calories: 246

Total fat: 23g

Protein: 7g

Total carbs: 8g

Fiber: 3g

Net carbs: 5g

Sodium: 49mg

Cholesterol: 3mg

Chocolate–Peanut Butter Fudge

Serves 12 • Prep: 10 minutes • Cook: 2 hours on low, plus 4 hours to chill

Rich, decadent chocolate–peanut butter fudge is easy to make in the slow cooker. This recipe is very versatile. You could substitute almond butter or hazelnut butter, or stir in chopped toasted nuts (peanuts, almonds, hazelnuts) at the end of the cooking time for variation. It cooks in just 2 hours and then needs to chill for at least another 4 before serving.

Coconut oil, for coating the slow cooker insert

1½ cups heavy (whipping) cream

1 cup all-natural peanut butter

1 tablespoon unsalted butter, melted

1 teaspoon pure vanilla extract

4 ounces unsweetened chocolate, chopped

½ cup erythritol

1 teaspoon stevia powder

1. Generously coat the inside of the slow cooker insert with coconut oil.

2. In the slow cooker, stir together the heavy cream, peanut butter, butter, vanilla, chocolate, erythritol, and stevia. Cover and cook for 2 hours on low, stirring occasionally.

3. Line a small, rimmed baking sheet with parchment or wax paper.

4. Transfer the cooked fudge to the prepared sheet and refrigerate for at least 4 hours.

5. Cut into squares and serve chilled.

Make It Paleo To make this recipe paleo, substitute almond butter for the peanut butter, coconut cream for the heavy cream, coconut oil for the butter, vanilla bean paste for the vanilla extract, and coconut sugar for the erythritol.

Fudge Nut Brownies

Makes 12 brownies • Prep: 15 minutes • Cook: 4 hours on low

QUICK PREP

PALEO FRIENDLY

These grain-free brownies are moist and rich. Two forms of chocolate give them deep chocolate flavor. Butter, cream, and mashed avocado keep them super moist.

¼ cup unsalted butter, plus more for coating the slow cooker insert

4 ounces unsweetened chocolate, chopped

1½ cups almond flour

½ cup unsweetened cocoa powder

¼ cup coconut flour

2 teaspoons baking powder

¼ teaspoon fine sea salt

1 large ripe avocado, peeled, pitted, and mashed

¼ cup heavy (whipping) cream

3 large eggs, lightly beaten

¾ cup erythritol

¾ teaspoon stevia powder

¾ cup coarsely chopped walnuts

Macronutrients
Fat 78%
Protein 9%
Carbs 13%

**Per Serving
(1 brownie)**
Calories: 229
Total fat: 21g
Protein: 6g
Total carbs: 10g
Fiber: 5g
Net carbs: 5g
Sodium: 75mg
Cholesterol: 70mg

1. Coat the bottom and sides of the slow cooker insert with butter, then line the bottom with parchment or wax paper (trace the bottom of the insert on the parchment and then cut it out).

2. In a small, microwave-safe bowl, combine ¼ cup of butter and the chocolate. Heat for 30-second intervals on high, stirring after each interval, until the chocolate is melted and the ingredients are fully incorporated.

3. In a medium bowl, stir together the almond flour, cocoa powder, coconut flour, baking powder, and salt.

4. In a large bowl, mix the avocado and heavy cream until smooth.

5. Add the eggs, erythritol, and stevia and mix to combine. Mix in the melted chocolate until incorporated.

6. Add the dry ingredients to the wet ingredients and mix until incorporated. Stir in the walnuts.

7. Transfer the mixture to the slow cooker and spread evenly. Cover and cook for 4 hours on low. Let cool for about 30 minutes in the slow cooker. Run a knife around the edge and then lift out of the insert. Cut into pieces and serve at room temperature.

Make It Paleo Substitute coconut oil for the butter, coconut milk for the heavy cream, and coconut sugar for the erythritol.

DESSERTS & SWEET TREATS

Macronutrients

Fat 80%

Protein 10%

Carbs 10%

Per Serving

Calories: 323

Total fat: 30g

Protein: 9g

Total carbs: 8g

Fiber: 3g

Net carbs: 5g

Sodium: 98mg

Cholesterol: 153mg

Chocolate Cake
with Whipped Cream

Serves 12 • Prep: 15 minutes • Cook: 3 hours on low

This rich, dark chocolate cake is perfect for special occasions. It takes just 3 hours to cook, but it keeps well in the refrigerator for up to 1 week or in the freezer for up to 3 months. If you're making it just for yourself, slice it into individual servings, wrap them in plastic wrap, and freeze. Thaw on the countertop before serving.

FOR THE CAKE

Coconut oil, for coating the slow cooker insert

1½ cups almond flour

¾ cup erythritol

⅔ cup unsweetened cocoa powder

¼ cup unflavored, unsweetened protein powder

2 teaspoons baking powder

¼ teaspoon fine sea salt

4 large eggs, lightly beaten

¾ cup canned coconut milk

½ cup (1 stick) unsalted butter, melted

1 teaspoon pure vanilla extract

½ cup chopped toasted hazelnuts

TO MAKE THE CAKE

1. Generously coat the inside of the slow cooker insert with coconut oil.

2. In a medium bowl, whisk together almond flour, erythritol, cocoa powder, protein powder, baking powder, and sea salt.

3. Stir in the eggs, coconut milk, butter, and vanilla until well mixed.

4. Gently fold in the hazelnuts. Transfer the batter to the prepared insert. Cover and cook for 3 hours on low.

FOR THE WHIPPED CREAM

1 cup heavy (whipping) cream

2 teaspoons stevia powder or
½ cup erythritol

1 teaspoon pure vanilla extract
or hazelnut extract

TO MAKE THE WHIPPED CREAM

1. In a large bowl, use an electric mixer set on medium-high to beat the heavy cream, stevia, and vanilla until stiff peaks form, about 5 minutes.

2. Turn off the slow cooker and let the cake cool for 30 minutes. Serve warm, topped with the whipped cream.

Make It Paleo Use almond milk or another dairy-free milk substitute and use coconut cream instead of heavy cream to make the whipped topping. Use vanilla bean paste in place of vanilla extract. Substitute coconut sugar for the erythritol.

EIGHT
Stocks, Condiments & Sauces

Macronutrients
Fat 0%
Protein 63%
Carbs 37%

Per Serving (1 cup)
Calories: 32
Total fat: 0g
Protein: 5g
Total carbs: 3g
Fiber: 0g
Net carbs: 3g
Sodium: 321mg
Cholesterol: 0mg

Beef Bone Broth

Makes 4 quarts • Prep: 15 minutes • Cook: 12 to 24 hours on low

Homemade bone broth makes a great flavor base for all sorts of rich soups, sauces, and stews, plus it's a nutritional powerhouse—full of collagen, essential amino acids, and minerals. For a different flavor, substitute lamb bones for the beef bones, or combine the two. You can substitute any type of acid for the apple cider vinegar, including freshly squeezed lemon juice, coconut vinegar, or wine vinegar, but don't skip it because the acid pulls those coveted minerals from the bones (don't worry; you won't taste it in the finished broth). The longer you let your broth cook, the more nutritious and flavorful it will be.

4 pounds beef bones

1 onion, roughly chopped

6 garlic cloves, peeled and smashed with the flat side of a knife

2 bay leaves

¼ cup apple cider vinegar

1 tablespoon kosher salt (optional)

4 quarts cold water

1. In the slow cooker, combine the beef bones, onion, garlic, bay leaves, cider vinegar, and salt (if using).

2. Pour in the water to cover. Cover and cook for at least 12 hours, and as long as 24 hours, on low. When finished, let cool.

3. Strain the broth through a fine-mesh sieve and discard the solids. Use immediately or transfer to jars and store in the refrigerator for up to 1 week or in the freezer for up to 3 months.

Variation Tip For a richer color and deeper flavor, roast the bones in a 375°F oven for 30 to 60 minutes before starting the broth.

Chicken Bone Broth

Makes 4 quarts • Prep: 10 minutes • Cook: 12 to 24 hours on low

QUICK PREP

ALLERGEN-FREE

PALEO FRIENDLY

MAKE AHEAD
IN BULK

Like beef bone broth, chicken bone broth is loaded with amino acids, collagen, and minerals. I always add chicken feet to my bone broth because they are mostly made of cartilage, which releases the gelatin that makes broth thick and rich. They're admittedly a bit creepy looking, so I understand if you don't want to use them. In that case, substitute an additional pound of chicken bones. Use this broth as a base for all sorts of soups, stews, and sauces, or just add some diced vegetables and shredded chicken for a simple, nourishing brew.

1 to 2 pounds chicken bones (2 to 3 chicken carcasses or an equal weight of assorted bones)

8 ounces chicken feet or 1 more pound of chicken bones

1 onion, roughly chopped

4 garlic cloves, peeled and smashed smashed with the flat side of a knife

2 celery stalks, cut into 3-inch pieces

2 bay leaves

2 tablespoons white wine vinegar

1 tablespoon kosher salt (optional)

4 quarts cold water

Macronutrients
Fat 22%
Protein 58%
Carbs 20%

Per Serving (1 cup)
Calories: 41
Total fat: 1g
Protein: 6g
Total carbs: 4g
Fiber: 0g
Net carbs: 4g
Sodium: 343mg
Cholesterol: 7mg

1. In the slow cooker, combine the chicken bones and feet, onion, garlic, celery, bay leaves, white wine vinegar, and salt (if using).

2. Pour in the water to cover. Cover and cook for at least 12 hours, and as long as 24 hours, on low. When finished, let cool.

3. Strain the broth through a fine-mesh sieve and discard the solids. Use immediately or transfer to jars and store in the refrigerator for up to 1 week or in the freezer for up to 3 months.

Variation Tip For a richer color and deeper flavor, roast the bones in a 375°F oven for 30 to 60 minutes before starting the broth.

STOCKS, CONDIMENTS & SAUCES

Macronutrients

Fat 39%

Protein 0%

Carbs 61%

Per Serving (1 cup)
Calories: 19
Total fat: 1g
Protein: 0g
Total carbs: 3g
Fiber: 0g
Net carbs: 3g
Sodium: 550mg
Cholesterol: 0mg

Vegetable Broth

Makes 4 quarts • Prep: 5 minutes • Cook: 8 to 12 hours on low

Purchased vegetable broth is often filled with unnecessary additives, but rich, delicious, highly nutritious, low-carb, and grain-free vegetable broth is easy to make in your slow cooker. Use this flavorful broth as a base for rich vegetarian soups, sauces, and stews. For a mushroom-flavored broth, substitute 12 ounces fresh mushrooms (or mushroom stems) for 2 of the onions and 2 of the celery stalks.

1 tablespoon extra-virgin olive oil

3 onions, quartered

3 celery stalks, cut into 3-inch pieces

6 garlic cloves, peeled and smashed with the flat side of a knife

1 bay leaf

1 tablespoon kosher salt (optional)

½ teaspoon black peppercorns

4 quarts water

1. In the slow cooker, combine the olive oil, onions, celery, garlic, bay leaf, salt (if using), and peppercorns.

2. Pour in the water. Cover and cook for 8 to 12 hours on low. When finished, let cool.

3. Strain the broth through a fine-mesh sieve and discard the solids. Use immediately or transfer to jars and store in the refrigerator for up to 5 days or in the freezer for up to 3 months.

Variation Tip For extra flavor, toss the vegetables with the olive oil on a rimmed baking sheet and roast in a 400°F oven for 45 to 60 minutes before starting the broth.

Condensed Cream of Mushroom Soup

Makes about 3 cups • Prep: 15 minutes • Cook: 4 hours on low or 2 hours on high

QUICK PREP

FASTER COOK OPTION

MAKE AHEAD IN BULK

How many times have you gotten halfway through the ingredients list of a great-looking recipe only to stumble upon the words, "1 can condensed cream of mushroom soup"? Make this version to use instead, which is all natural and keto friendly, and you can finally make all those delicious-sounding recipes with a clear conscience. You can even use it as a sauce just by adding a bit more cream or broth. One batch makes the equivalent of two cans of condensed soup. To serve this as a soup, add 2 cups water or Vegetable Broth (page 176) and heat over medium heat.

½ cup (1 stick) unsalted butter or Ghee (page 179)

1 medium onion, chopped

2 garlic cloves, minced

1 pound sliced mushrooms

1 cup dry white wine

2 cups Vegetable Broth (page 176)

1 fresh thyme sprig

1½ teaspoons kosher salt

1½ teaspoons freshly ground black pepper

4 ounces cream cheese

¾ cup heavy (whipping) cream

Macronutrients
Fat 83%
Protein 8%
Carbs 9%

Per Serving (½ cup)
Calories: 304
Total fat: 28g
Protein: 6g
Total carbs: 7g
Fiber: 1g
Net carbs: 6g
Sodium: 1014mg
Cholesterol: 82mg

1. In a large skillet, melt the butter over medium-high heat. Add the onion and garlic and sauté until softened, about 5 minutes.

2. Add the mushrooms and sauté until softened, about 3 minutes more.

3. Stir in the white wine, bring to a boil, and cook for 2 more minutes. Transfer the vegetables to the slow cooker.

4. Stir in the vegetable broth, thyme, salt, and pepper. Cover and cook for 4 hours on low or 2 hours on high.

5. When finished, discard the thyme sprig and use an immersion blender or a countertop blender to purée the soup (half or all of it).

6. Stir in the cream cheese and heavy cream. Use immediately or transfer to jars and keep refrigerated for up to 1 week.

Variation Tip If you want to make a large batch for future use, leave out the cream cheese and heavy cream initially. Freeze in two equal portions for up to 3 months. Add 2 ounces cream cheese and 6 tablespoons heavy cream to each portion after thawing and before using in a recipe.

STOCKS, CONDIMENTS & SAUCES

Macronutrients
Fat 0%
Protein 0%
Carbs 100%

**Per Serving
(2 tablespoons)**
Calories: 8
Total fat: 0g
Protein: 0g
Total carbs: 2g
Fiber: 0g
Net carbs: 2g
Sodium: 152mg
Cholesterol: 0mg

Easy Keto Ketchup

Makes about 2 cups • Prep: 10 minutes • Cook: 8 hours on low

Commercial ketchup is loaded with sugar. This sugar-free slow cooker version is low in net carbs but still packed with flavor. Enjoy it on burgers, use it to flavor meatloaf, or even put it on your eggs if you're into that.

1 cup tomato purée

1 small onion, chopped

2 garlic cloves, chopped

¼ cup water

¼ cup apple cider vinegar or wine vinegar (red or white)

3 to 6 drops stevia extract

2 tablespoons erythritol or ⅓ teaspoon stevia powder

1 teaspoon kosher salt

⅓ teaspoon ground allspice

⅓ teaspoon ground cloves

Pinch freshly ground black pepper

1. In the slow cooker, stir together the tomato purée, onion, garlic, water, vinegar, stevia extract, erythritol, salt, allspice, cloves, and pepper. Cover and cook for 8 hours on low.

2. When finished, use an immersion blender or a countertop blender to purée the ketchup until smooth.

3. Refrigerate in an airtight container for up to 3 weeks.

Variation Tip For a spicy ketchup, add cayenne pepper to the mix along with the other spices. Start with ¼ teaspoon and add more to suit your personal tastes.

Ghee

Makes about 2 cups • Prep: 10 minutes • Cook: 2 to 3 hours on low

Ghee, a common ingredient in Indian cuisine, is clarified butter, meaning that it is cooked for a very long time until the fat separates from the solids, and then strained, removing the milk solids, sugars, and water. What's left is only the fat or oil. Since most dairy-intolerant people react to the proteins or carbohydrates in butter, ghee can be a great substitute (trace amounts of proteins or carbs may be present, so extremely sensitive people should avoid it). And, because the milk solids have been removed, many who follow a paleo diet have embraced this flavorful fat. The long cooking time gives it an irresistible nutty aroma and flavor. Like coconut oil, ghee has a high smoke point (485°F), lasts a long time, and delivers complex toasted butter flavor. Use ghee as a replacement for butter, coconut oil, and other fats. Though available commercially, ghee is easy to make in a slow cooker. You'll need cheesecloth and a funnel or a very fine-mesh sieve.

1 pound (4 sticks) unsalted butter

1. Put the butter in the slow cooker.

2. Cover the slow cooker, but set the lid ajar (you can prop a chopstick or wooden spoon underneath) to allow steam to escape. Cook for 2 to 3 hours on low, until the milk solids separate from the fat. You'll notice that the solids have begun to brown, fall to the bottom, and stick to the sides of the pot. The surface of the butter will also bubble and foam as the water boils off.

3. Line a funnel with cheesecloth and place it over a jar or other storage container. If you are using a sieve, place the sieve over the jar. Slowly pour the oil through the cheesecloth or sieve. Let cool to room temperature before sealing the container.

4. For best results, refrigerate, where it will last for months.

Make It Paleo To make ghee that is acceptable for those following a paleo diet, use only organic butter from grass-fed cows.

Macronutrients
Fat 100%
Protein 0%
Carbs 0%

**Per Serving
(1 tablespoon)**
Calories: 112
Total fat: 13g
Protein: 0g
Total carbs: 0g
Fiber: 0g
Net carbs: 0g
Sodium: 0mg
Cholesterol: 33mg

STOCKS, CONDIMENTS & SAUCES

QUICK PREP

FASTER COOK
OPTION

ALLERGEN-FREE

PALEO FRIENDLY

MAKE AHEAD
IN BULK

Macronutrients
Fat 51%
Protein 20%
Carbs 29%

Per Serving (¼ cup)
Calories: 41
Total fat: 3g
Protein: 2g
Total carbs: 3g
Fiber: 1g
Net carbs: 1g
Sodium: 319mg
Cholesterol: 5mg

Enchilada Sauce

Makes about 3 cups • Prep: 5 minutes • Cook: 8 hours on low or 4 hours on high

Most enchilada sauces are thickened with flour or other starchy thickeners, but this one is grain-free and very low in net carbs. And the best thing is it's a total fix-it-and-forget-it recipe. Just stir the ingredients together in the slow cooker, cover, and let it cook all day. Choose a hot, medium, or mild chili powder to suit your taste. You can use this rich, spicy sauce in low-carb casseroles, to top fried eggs, or as a sauce for meat, chicken, or fish. To bump up the fat content, stir in 1 cup sour cream before using.

3 cups chicken broth

3 tablespoons tomato paste

2 tablespoons Ghee (page 179), unsalted butter, or coconut oil

1 bay leaf

¼ cup pure chili powder

2 teaspoons ground cumin

1 teaspoon dried oregano

½ teaspoon kosher salt

½ teaspoon garlic powder

½ teaspoon onion powder

½ teaspoon erythritol (optional)

¼ teaspoon ground chipotle

Pinch ground cloves

Pinch ground cinnamon

1. In the slow cooker, stir together all the ingredients.

2. Cover and cook for 8 hours on low or 4 hours on high. If possible, stir the sauce once or twice during cooking.

3. Discard the bay leaf. Use the sauce immediately or cool to room temperature and then freeze it in an airtight container for up to 3 months.

Variation Tip If you want a thicker consistency, when the cooking is finished, sprinkle in ¼ to ½ teaspoon xanthan gum and whisk to blend thoroughly into the sauce.

Creamy Tomato Sauce

Makes about 5 cups • Prep: 10 minutes • Cook: 6 hours on low or 3 hours on high

Jarred tomato sauces are a dime a dozen and most contain added sugar, and many also contain starchy emulsifiers, thickeners, and other undesirable ingredients. This version has no added sugar or thickeners. Serve this rich, creamy sauce over zucchini noodles or spaghetti squash, or as a sauce for meatballs, meatloaf, or chicken.

1 (28-ounce) can diced tomatoes, with juice

¼ cup tomato paste

¼ cup Ghee (page 179), unsalted butter, or coconut oil

2 tablespoons red wine vinegar

1 teaspoon onion powder

1 teaspoon garlic powder

1 teaspoon dried basil

1 teaspoon dried oregano

1 teaspoon dried parsley

1 teaspoon kosher salt

½ teaspoon red pepper flakes

¼ teaspoon freshly ground black pepper

1 cup heavy (whipping) cream

Macronutrients
Fat 72%
Protein 7%
Carbs 21%

Per Serving (½ cup)
Calories: 113
Total fat: 9g
Protein: 2g
Total carbs: 6g
Fiber: 2g
Net carbs: 4g
Sodium: 446mg
Cholesterol: 29mg

1. In the slow cooker, stir together the tomatoes and their juice, tomato paste, ghee, red wine vinegar, onion and garlic powders, basil, oregano, parsley, salt, red pepper flakes, and black pepper. Cover and cook for 6 hours on low or 3 hours on high.

2. When finished, use an immersion blender or a countertop blender to purée the sauce.

3. Stir in the heavy cream. Serve immediately or refrigerate in an airtight container for up to 3 days.

Variation Tip If you want to make a large batch for future use, omit the cream initially. You can refrigerate the sauce without the cream for up to 1 week or freeze it for up to 3 months. Add the cream after reheating the sauce, just before serving.

STOCKS, CONDIMENTS & SAUCES

Macronutrients

Fat 87%

Protein 10%

Carbs 3%

Per Serving (¼ cup)

Calories: 165

Total fat: 16g

Protein: 4g

Total carbs: 1g

Fiber: 0g

Net carbs: 1g

Sodium: 171mg

Cholesterol: 50mg

Spicy Cheese Sauce or Dip

Makes about 2 ¼ cups • Prep: 5 minutes • Cook: 30 to 60 minutes on low

This sauce is quick and easy to make. It makes a lot and keeps for up to 1 week refrigerated, so you can make a batch and use it for several meals. Serve it as a dip for vegetables or over low-carb nachos. Or thin it with a bit of extra cream and use it as a sauce for steamed vegetables, zucchini noodles, or spaghetti squash.

1 cup shredded sharp Cheddar cheese

½ cup heavy (whipping) cream

½ cup cream cheese

¼ cup Ghee (page 179) or unsalted butter

½ teaspoon cayenne pepper

½ teaspoon garlic powder

½ teaspoon onion powder

½ teaspoon paprika

Pinch kosher salt

1. In the slow cooker, stir together all the ingredients.

2. Cover and cook for 30 to 60 minutes on low. Whisk, if needed, to combine.

3. Serve hot, or cool to room temperature and refrigerate for up to 1 week. Reheat in the top of a double boiler or in 30-second intervals on high in the microwave.

Variation Tip Make a chorizo cheese dip by browning 8 ounces chorizo in a skillet and adding it to the slow cooker in step 1.

Gorgonzola Cream Sauce

Makes about 3 cups • Prep: 5 minutes • Cook 30 to 60 minutes on low

QUICK PREP

MAKE AHEAD
IN BULK

While not an all-day-slow-cook recipe, this rich sauce is incredibly simple to make. Just combine the ingredients in the slow cooker and let it cook for 30 to 60 minutes. Serve it tossed with zucchini noodles, spaghetti squash, or steamed vegetables, or spoon it over chicken or steak.

2 cups heavy (whipping) cream

1⅓ cups Gorgonzola cheese

½ cup grated Parmesan cheese

½ teaspoon freshly ground black pepper

1. In the slow cooker, stir together all the ingredients.

2. Cover and cook for 30 to 60 minutes on low. Whisk, if needed, to combine. Serve hot.

Variation Tip You can substitute any kind of cheese you like for the Gorgonzola. Also, add more flavor with fresh herbs, such as rosemary, parsley, or oregano. Stir them in at the end of the cooking time.

Macronutrients
Fat 79%
Protein 15%
Carbs 6%

Per Serving (¼ cup)
Calories: 158
Total fat: 14g
Protein: 6g
Total carbs: 2g
Fiber: 1g
Net carbs: 1g
Sodium: 288mg
Cholesterol: 48mg

STOCKS, CONDIMENTS & SAUCES

Macronutrients

Fat 77%

Protein 7%

Carbs 6%

Per Serving

(2 tablespoons)

Calories: 70

Total fat: 6g

Protein: 3g

Total carbs: 2g

Fiber: 0g

Net carbs: 2g

Sodium: 93mg

Cholesterol: 15mg

Creamy Spinach-Cheese Spread

Makes about 3 cups • Prep: 5 minutes • Cook: 4 hours on low or 2 hours on high

Whether slathered on a steak or scooped up with raw veggies, this creamy, spinach-cheese concoction is a sure winner. Serve it as a dip for low-carb veggies, as a sauce on grilled meats, or as a filling or spread for low-carb wraps.

Unsalted butter, Ghee (page 179), or extra-virgin olive oil, for coating the slow cooker insert

10 ounces baby spinach, chopped

8 ounces cream cheese, cut into small pieces

¾ cup sour cream

¼ cup mayonnaise

½ cup grated Parmesan cheese

½ teaspoon red pepper flakes

¼ teaspoon garlic powder

¼ teaspoon kosher salt

¼ teaspoon freshly ground black pepper

1. Generously coat the inside of the slow cooker insert with butter.

2. Add the spinach, cream cheese, sour cream, mayonnaise, Parmesan cheese, red pepper flakes, garlic powder, salt, and pepper.

3. Cover and cook for 4 hours on low or 2 hours on high. Stir to combine. Serve hot. The spread can be refrigerated for up to 5 days.

Variation Tip For a festive party presentation, transfer the spread to a baking dish, sprinkle additional Parmesan cheese over the top, and broil until the top is bubbly and golden, 3 to 4 minutes.

Sweet Blueberry Syrup

Makes about 2 ½ cups • Prep: 5 minutes • Cook: 4 hours on low or 2 hours on high

This sweet syrup is the perfect way to brighten up low-carb pancakes or crêpes. It's also delicious as a dessert sauce drizzled over low-carb ice cream or cake or stirred into full-fat yogurt or ricotta cheese for a simple treat. Note that on its own this syrup is mostly carbs, so enjoy it as a topping for high-fat dishes, such as ice cream or cake.

1 cup frozen blueberries

1 cup water

2 teaspoons freshly squeezed lemon juice

½ cup erythritol or ½ teaspoon stevia powder

¼ teaspoon xanthan gum

½ teaspoon pure vanilla extract (optional)

1. In the slow cooker, mix the blueberries, water, lemon juice, and erythritol. Cover and cook for 4 hours on low or 2 hours on low. Whisk to combine.

2. Transfer ½ cup of the syrup to a small bowl. Whisk in the xanthan gum until very well incorporated. Whisk the mixture back into the syrup in the slow cooker.

3. Whisk in the vanilla (if using).

4. Serve warm or chilled. Store the sauce in an airtight container in the refrigerator for up to 1 week or in the freezer for up to 3 months.

Variation Tip Substitute any berry you like for the blueberries in this recipe or use a combination of berries, but you may want to strain out any seeds, especially if you use raspberries.

Macronutrients
Fat 6%
Protein 4%
Carbs 90%

Per Serving (¼ cup)
Calories: 14
Total fat: 0g
Protein: 0g
Total carbs: 4g
Fiber: 0g
Net carbs: 4g
Sodium: 0mg
Cholesterol: 0mg

STOCKS, CONDIMENTS & SAUCES

Macronutrients
Fat 97%
Protein 1%
Carbs 2%

**Per Serving
(2 tablespoons)**
Calories: 114
Total fat: 13g
Protein: 0g
Total carbs: 1g
Fiber: 0g
Net carbs: 1g
Sodium: 14mg
Cholesterol: 41mg

Rich Caramel Sauce

Makes about 2 cups • Prep: 5 minutes • Cook: 8 hours on low

I didn't believe it was possible until I tried it myself, but it turns out you can make a delectable caramel sauce without sugar. This low-carb version is every bit as rich and delicious as the caramel you've been missing. For a different flavor, substitute maple extract for the vanilla. Serve this drizzled over low-carb ice cream, spooned over low-carb cake, or stirred into your morning coffee (yes, please!).

1¼ cups heavy (whipping) cream

1 cup brown sugar erythritol blend (such as Sukrin Gold) or 1 cup erythritol plus 2 teaspoons blackstrap molasses

½ cup (1 stick) unsalted butter or Ghee (page 179)

Pinch fine sea salt

¼ teaspoon xanthan gum

½ teaspoon pure vanilla extract

1. In the slow cooker, combine the heavy cream, brown sugar erythritol blend, butter, and sea salt. Cover and cook for 8 hours on low. When finished, whisk the mixture to combine.

2. Transfer ½ cup of the sauce to a small bowl. Whisk in the xanthan gum until very well incorporated. Whisk the mixture back into the sauce in the slow cooker.

3. Whisk in the vanilla.

4. Transfer the sauce to a bowl or jar and let cool. It will thicken as it cools.

5. Serve warm. Refrigerate any leftovers for up to 1 week or freeze for up to 3 months. Reheat in 30-second intervals on high in the microwave.

Variation Tip To make a thicker caramel, after adding the xanthan gum, turn the slow cooker to high and let the caramel cook, uncovered, for 30 minutes more, whisking occasionally. Whisk in the vanilla and let cool.

Dreamy Hot Chocolate Sauce

Makes about 3 cups • Prep: 5 minutes • Cook: 1 hour

This rich, chocolaty sauce is truly a dream come true for those following a low-carb, high-fat diet. It's sugar free, with only a few grams of net carbs per serving. It's delicious drizzled over berries, low-carb ice cream, or low-carb cake. Or, you know, just eaten with a spoon (you know you want to).

2 cups heavy (whipping) cream

4 ounces unsweetened chocolate, finely chopped

⅔ cup erythritol

1 teaspoon pure vanilla extract

1. In the slow cooker, combine the heavy cream, chocolate, and erythritol. Cover and cook for 1 hour on low. When finished, stir to combine.

2. Whisk in the vanilla. Serve hot.

3. Refrigerate leftovers for up to 1 week. Reheat the sauce in the slow cooker, in the top of a double boiler, or in the microwave in 30-second intervals on high.

Make It Allergen-Free/Paleo To make this sauce both paleo and allergen-free, substitute full-fat coconut milk for the heavy cream. For paleo, also substitute vanilla bean paste for the vanilla extract and coconut sugar for the erythritol.

ACKNOWLEDGEMENTS

Thank you to my husband, Doug Reil, for his constant support and encouragement and, especially, for indulging my passion for writing cookbooks. Thanks, also, to my son, Cashel, for giving me the best reason to get up every morning, and for being willing to try so many of my kitchen experiments.

I am also grateful to the editorial team at Callisto Media including, but not limited to, Clara Song Lee, Talia Platz, Stacey Wagner-Kinnear, and Jenny Croghan for their dedication, professionalism, and commitment to creating high-quality content.

Appendix A

MEASUREMENT CONVERSIONS

Volume Equivalents (Liquid)

US STANDARD	US STANDARD (OUNCES)	METRIC (APPROXIMATE)
2 tablespoons	1 fl. oz.	30 mL
¼ cup	2 fl. oz.	60 mL
½ cup	4 fl. oz.	120 mL
1 cup	8 fl. oz.	240 mL
1½ cups	12 fl. oz.	355 mL
2 cups or 1 pint	16 fl. oz.	475 mL
4 cups or 1 quart	32 fl. oz.	1 L
1 gallon	128 fl. oz.	4 L

Oven Temperatures

FAHRENHEIT	CELSIUS (APPROXIMATE)
250°F	120°C
300°F	150°C
325°F	165°C
350°F	180°C
375°F	190°C
400°F	200°C
425°F	220°C
450°F	230°C

Volume Equivalents (Dry)

US STANDARD	METRIC (APPROXIMATE)
⅛ teaspoon	0.5 mL
¼ teaspoon	1 mL
½ teaspoon	2 mL
¾ teaspoon	4 mL
1 teaspoon	5 mL
1 tablespoon	15 mL
¼ cup	59 mL
⅓ cup	79 mL
½ cup	118 mL
⅔ cup	156 mL
¾ cup	177 mL
1 cup	235 mL
2 cups or 1 pint	475 mL
3 cups	700 mL
4 cups or 1 quart	1 L

Weight Equivalents

US STANDARD	METRIC (APPROXIMATE)
½ ounce	15 g
1 ounce	30 g
2 ounces	60 g
4 ounces	115 g
8 ounces	225 g
12 ounces	340 g
16 ounces or 1 pound	455 g

THE DIRTY DOZEN & THE CLEAN FIFTEEN

A nonprofit environmental watchdog organization called Environmental Working Group (EWG) looks at data supplied by the US Department of Agriculture (USDA) and the Food and Drug Administration (FDA) about pesticide residues. Each year it compiles a list of the best and worst pesticide loads found in commercial crops. You can use these lists to decide which fruits and vegetables to buy organic to minimize your exposure to pesticides and which produce is considered safe enough to buy conventionally. This does not mean they are pesticide-free, though, so wash these fruits and vegetables thoroughly.

These lists change every year, so make sure you look up the most recent one before you fill your shopping cart. You'll find the most recent lists, as well as a guide to pesticides in produce, at EWG.org/FoodNews.

Dirty Dozen

Apples	Nectarines	*In addition to the Dirty Dozen, the EWG added two types of produce contaminated with highly toxic organo-phosphate insecticides:*
Celery	Peaches	
Cherries	Spinach	
Cherry tomatoes	Strawberries	
Cucumbers	Sweet bell peppers	Kale/Collard greens
Grapes	Tomatoes	Hot peppers

Clean Fifteen

Asparagus	Eggplant	Onions
Avocados	Grapefruit	Papayas
Cabbage	Honeydew Melon	Pineapples
Cantaloupe	Kiwis	Sweet corn
Cauliflower	Mangos	Sweet peas (frozen)

RECIPE INDEX

INDEX

ABOUT THE AUTHOR

Robin Donovan is a food and nutrition writer and recipe developer. She is co-author of the *New York Times* bestseller, *Dr. Gott's No Flour, No Sugar Diet*, and the author of numerous cookbooks, including *Campfire Cuisine: Gourmet Recipes for the Great Outdoors* and *The Lazy Gourmet: Magnificent Meals Made Easy*. Her food writing has appeared in *Cooking Light, Fitness, San Jose Mercury News, San Francisco Chronicle*, and elsewhere. She lives in the San Francisco Bay Area with her husband and son and blogs about super easy recipes for delicious and healthy meals at www.TwoLazyGourmets.com.

CPSIA information can be obtained
at www.ICGtesting.com
Printed in the USA
BVOW07s2109150716
455649BV00003B/4/P

9 781623 157715